I0189114

IMAGES
of America

BOTETOURT
COUNTY

Botetourt County residents were heartbroken when they awoke on the frosty morning of December 15, 1970, to find that their historic courthouse had burned. This photograph shows the beginning of the rebuilding efforts, which necessitated the dismantling of the brick walls. (Courtesy of the *Fincastle Herald*.)

ON THE COVER: The Eagle Rock Limestone Company operated from 1905 to 1954. This 1917 photograph shows construction underway for the fourth kiln stack at the plant. Among those pictured are owners James and Helen McNamara, who are standing together on the roof. The frame structure at the far left is the support for the "dinky" rail line that brought limestone from the quarry to the kilns. (Courtesy of Ray and Bobbie Sloan.)

IMAGES
of America

BOTETOURT COUNTY

Debra Alderson McClane

ARCADIA
PUBLISHING

Copyright © 2007 by Debra Alderson McClane
ISBN 978-1-5316-2668-6

Published by Arcadia Publishing
Charleston, South Carolina

Library of Congress Catalog Card Number: 2006932457

For all general information contact Arcadia Publishing at:
Telephone 843-853-2070
Fax 843-853-0044
E-mail sales@arcadiapublishing.com
For customer service and orders:
Toll-Free 1-888-313-2665

Visit us on the Internet at www.arcadiapublishing.com

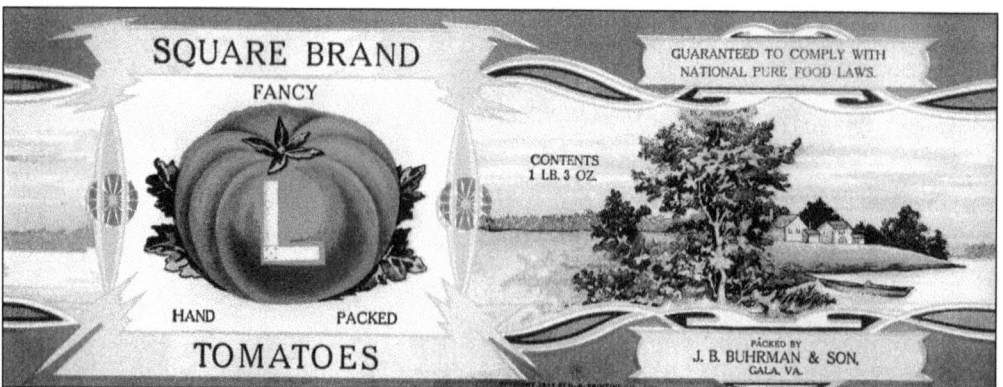

Beginning in the late 19th century, the production of fruits and vegetables for market, or "trucking," became a mainstay of the agricultural economy in Botetourt County. Factories on nearly every farm canned items such as peaches, green beans, and tomatoes. Most factories closed during the 1940s. This 1911 canning label is from the "Square Brand" of the Joseph B. Buhrman farm in Gala. (Courtesy of Joseph B. Buhrman.)

CONTENTS

ACKNOWLEDGMENTS

There are several individuals who assisted me in my searches at various libraries and museums. I would like to thank Patty King and Weldon Martin at the Botetourt County Historical Museum; Jane Wills at the Digital Library and Archives at Virginia Polytechnic Institute and State University; Harry Hubbard and his staff (including Lauren and Josh) and Michael B. Barber at the Virginia Department of Historic Resources; Lynn Bolton and Peggy Crosson at Historic Fincastle, Inc.; Ed McCoy at the *Fincastle Herald*; Harry Gleason, Downtown Revitalization director, Town of Buchanan; Tommy Moore and Loretta Caldwell at the Botetourt County Clerk's Office; Dana Angell at the Library of Virginia; Jackie Holt at the Blue Ridge Parkway, National Park Service; John Regan at the U.S. Army Corps of Engineers; and Barry LeNoir at Camp Bethel.

Individuals who shared their private collections and insights with me include Edna Brogan Bolton, Joseph B. Buhrman, Darys Caldwell Cahoon, Clyde and Beulah Chambers, Eugene Crotty, Ronnie and Melinda Firestone, Rita Firestone, Mrs. E. A. Graybill Jr., Katherine Camper Harris, John R. Hildebrand Jr., Pat Honts, Sidney Hunter, Malanie Jones, Antonia Wood McCoy, Tom Myers, Josephine Zimmerman Noojin, Geraldine Mangus Obenshain, Darlene Odenwelder, Betty Jeter Painter, Bland Painter, Greg Rieley, Ray and Bobbie Sloan, and Dorothy Vernamonti. Each of these people contributed to this book and in doing so have helped to preserve a piece of the county's rich history. I am grateful to all who willingly shared their images, stories, and knowledge about the county.

Thanks also go to the two editors who helped me with this project: Kathryn Korfonta and Courtney Hutton.

I also would like to thank my husband, Patrick, for his patience during yet another of my many projects. Most of all, I thank my parents, John and Doris Alderson, who have greatly assisted me in gathering these images.

Photograph courtesies from Norfolk and Western Historical Photograph Collection and the Virginia Cooperative Extensive Service Collection, which are part of the Digital Library and Archives, University Libraries, Virginia Polytechnic and State University, are abbreviated as NWHP, DLA, VPISU and VCESC, DLA, VPISU.

INTRODUCTION

In collecting images for this book, I have tried to represent as many of the localities in the county as possible. My work has been guided by historians who have come before me, notably Robert Douthat Stoner, whose *A Seed-Bed of the Republic* remains the most comprehensive county history to date. Others, whose names you will find in the bibliography, pointed me to significant places, people, and events.

Historically known as a gateway to the west, Botetourt County, located in the southwestern part of Virginia at the southern end of the Shenandoah Valley, is bounded by the Alleghany and the Blue Ridge Mountains. Centuries before European explorers and settlers discovered the area, Native American tribes lived and prospered here. Located at the heavily traveled crossroads of major trails, the inhabitants of Southwestern Virginia were influenced by numerous tribes and cultural affiliations that resulted in a unique blending of cultural attributes. Artifacts recovered at numerous archaeological sites in Botetourt show these cultural influences in pottery and ceramics, as well as in burial practices.

By 1730, as settlements in this part of the state were established, most of the native tribes had moved west or had died out. European settlements were sparse until after the end of the French and Indian War. Among them were German and Scots-Irish settlers who traveled to the area from Pennsylvania and Maryland along the Great Wagon Road or Valley Road. English settlers arrived from the east, and a few early settlers were French Huguenots.

In 1770, Botetourt County was created from lands that were formerly part of Augusta County. As the county developed, people used place names to characterize and to identify their new homes. In Botetourt, some of these names were derived from the setting in which the community existed, such as Arcadia, Alpine, Blue Ridge, Cloverdale, Silent Dell, and Solitude. Other place names were rooted in the mineral industry, like Bessemer, Iron Gate, Lignite, Pico, and Spec. Like the county itself, places also were named for people, including Buchanan, Fincastle, Troutville, Glen Wilton, Hickory, and Houston. The residents also defined "home" by the creeks and mountains that surrounded them, such as Back Creek, Catawba Creek, Craig Creek, Glade Creek, Jennings Creek, Lapsley's Run, Mill Creek, North Creek, Bald Mountain, Caldwell Mountain, Cove Mountain, Crawford Mountain, Price Mountain, Purgatory Mountain, Tinker Mountain, and Rathole Mountain.

Citizens in the young county answered the call during war beginning in the 18th century with the French and Indian War and the American Revolution. War heroes Andrew Lewis and William Fleming were Botetourt residents. During the Revolution, many of Botetourt's farmers provided troops with horses and supplies. During the Civil War, Botetourt mustered 12 full companies into service for the Confederate army. Some of the county's African American residents joined Union troops, including Pleasant Richardson, who served with the U.S. 45th Colored Troops, and John William Camper, who was killed on his way home from the war in 1865. Many of the county's men and women also contributed service during 20th-century conflicts.

The first half of the 19th century was a prosperous time for the county. With an economy based on agriculture, associated industries soon developed, including blacksmiths, wheelwrights, tanneries, and, most importantly, mills. Significant crops included hemp, wheat, and corn. Tobacco was grown but was not as significant a crop as it was in the east, since the soils and geography here were more suited to raising livestock and to producing grains and hay. Iron furnaces began to thrive off of the county's rich deposits of brown and red hematite ores. Limestone and marble mining soon followed. With increased industry and new and improved transportation routes, including turnpike roads and the arrival of the James River and Kanawha Canal in 1851, county residents fashioned a good living in the surrounding valleys and hills.

The Civil War brought a halt to this prosperity, but soon afterwards, residents returned to agricultural, industrial, and commercial pursuits. Farms diversified and new endeavors included apple and peach orchards, dairying, and vegetable and fruit production for market. In the 20th century, mechanization of farm equipment replaced human labor with motor-driven labor and made county farms more efficient and productive.

In the late 19th century, the railroad also arrived in the county. The major lines of the Chesapeake and Ohio (C&O) and the Norfolk and Western (N&W) eventually took over the smaller lines. The Roanoke, Fincastle, and Clifton Forge Railroad was planned to traverse the county from Fincastle to Cloverdale and to connect to the C&O in Roanoke, but the line never materialized, leaving Fincastle without a railroad connection.

Another important economic activity during the late 19th century was the commercial development of mineral springs resorts with hotels that offered entertainment, shopping, and dining. Among the popular springs localities were Fincastle, Blue Ridge, Coyner's, Dagger's, and Lithia.

Churches, schools, and social organizations also played an important role in the lives of the residents. Many of Botetourt's early settlers were religious dissenters—that is, they were not members of the established church of England. Denominations represented early on in the county include Baptists, Presbyterians, Lutherans, Methodists, and German Baptists (later, Church of the Brethren).

Private schools and academies, church schools, and home schools first provided educational instruction to county children. A free school system was established locally in 1846, with numerous schools being built in small communities. One-room schools later were consolidated into larger schools that taught elementary and high school curricula. Elementary education was provided separately for African American children; only Academy Hill in Fincastle offered grades 1 through 12. In 1959, Botetourt built Central Academy, which provided a full secondary education for black students countywide. In 1966, Botetourt schools were integrated.

The county's natural resources and beauty are the underlying characteristics that define what Botetourt truly is. The topography and geography of the land has been the prime influencing factor in everything from settlement patterns to transportation routes in this county.

The following images help to illustrate the history of the county from traces of its native inhabitants through the late 20th century. The people, places, and events depicted here are reflective of the hardworking breed that established this place on the late-18th century frontier. Their names and the institutions they founded, and hopefully some of their spirit, continues to live here.

One

BEGINNINGS

As early as 1767, a petition was made to the Virginia House of Burgesses to create a new county by division of Augusta County. In December 1769, the General Assembly assented, and on February 13, 1770, the Botetourt County Court held its first meeting at Robert Breckenridge's home near Daleville. The county was named in honor of Norborne Berkeley, Baron de Botetourt, of Gloucestershire, who was royal governor of the Virginia colony from 1768 to 1770. The original county boundaries stretched from the Blue Ridge Mountains in the east to the Mississippi River in the west. As settlements in the west increased, that land was organized into new counties in Virginia, West Virginia, Ohio, Indiana, Illinois, and Wisconsin. The entire state of Kentucky was at one time part of Botetourt County. Today Botetourt County encompasses roughly 550 square miles and has a population of about 31,000. (Courtesy of John R. Hildebrand Jr.)

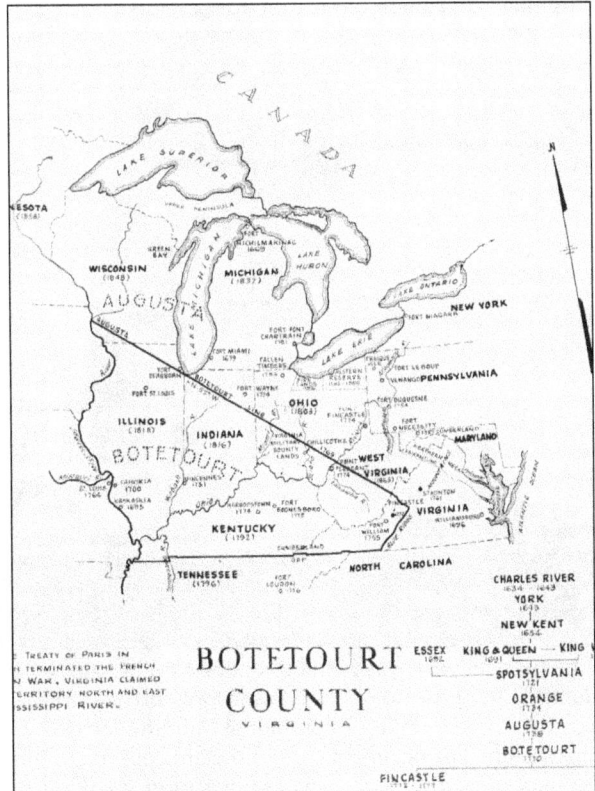

When Europeans arrived in the 1730s, most of the original inhabitants had left the area, and the land was claimed by several tribes as a hunting ground. Evidence of early inhabitants was found at the Bessemer Archaeological Site on the western floodplain of the James River, near Eagle Rock (above). Artifacts indicate that the site was occupied from the Late Woodland period (about 1000 AD) through the mid-15th century by two different aboriginal cultures. (Courtesy of Virginia Department of Historic Resources.)

The Bessemer site was found to contain numerous Native American hearths, middens (or trash dumps), and post holes. The latter formed the outline of a long structure with rounded ends, possibly a ceremonial or communal building located within a palisaded village, as depicted in this sketch. The occupants of the site are believed to have returned on a seasonal basis and were hunters and gatherers, as well as horticulturists. (Courtesy of Thomas Whyte.)

In 1759, William Preston Sr. purchased from Stephen Renfroe property that was located north of Amsterdam. Soon Preston had constructed a frame dwelling that he called Greenfield (above). The house burned in 1959, but archaeological remains of the structure are intact at the site, as are three cemeteries and several log structures. In 1995, the county purchased Greenfield for development as a business complex. (Courtesy of Virginia Department of Historic Resources.)

Prior to European settlement at Greenfield, numerous Native American groups passed through the area and may have created a seasonal encampment along the intermittent streams on the land. Archaeological evidence suggests that aboriginal occupation occurred at this site from about 8000 BC to the late 1600s. This collection of tools, points, ceramics, and soapstone pieces illustrates the variety of materials found at the property. (Courtesy of Botetourt County, Virginia Department of Historic Resources.)

In 1783, William Preston died at his Montgomery County home, Smithfield. His son John inherited the land at Greenfield, which passed to his children. John's daughter Sarah married Henry M. Bowyer, and by the 1850s, they had constructed a brick house on her portion of the farm (above). In 1802, Louis and Virginia Holladay purchased the property. The house, which featured a tall columned porch, was destroyed around 1975. (Courtesy of Virginia Department of Historic Resources.)

Archaeological investigations at the Bowyer-Holladay House site (above) provide insight into the construction of the dwelling and the material culture of those who lived there. Greenfield was a large farm within a society of mostly smaller farms and as such reflected a more prosperous existence. At one time, part of William Preston's late-18th-century, 2,100-acre holdings, Greenfield was actively farmed into the 20th century. (Courtesy of Botetourt County, Virginia Department of Historic Resources.)

Lord Botetourt, who lived in Virginia when he was governor, was popular with the colonists and was a "friend and patron" of the College of William and Mary. After his death, a statue of his likeness was placed in the piazza in front of the Capitol in Williamsburg. The marble statue (right), damaged during various moves, is housed in the Swem Library, and a bronze replica is located in the College Yard. Botetourt is buried in the college's Wren Chapel. (Courtesy of the College of William and Mary.)

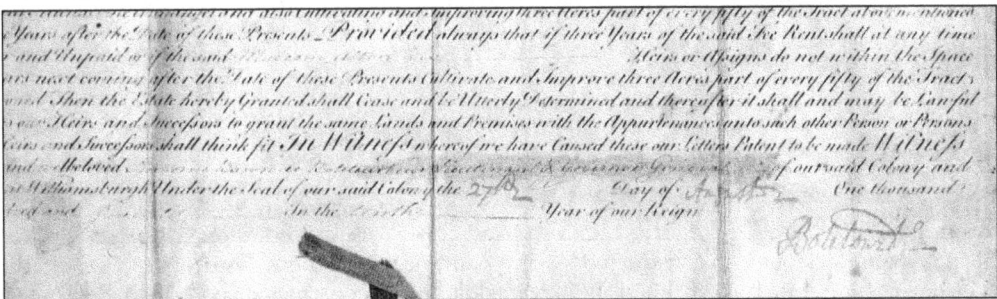

Lord Botetourt's signature is seen on this 1770 grant of land to Malcom Allen, who first patented land at the western end of Purgatory Mountain in 1754. Among the wealth of historical documents held at the Botetourt Courthouse are documents signed by Lord Dunmore, the last royal governor of the colony. (Courtesy of Botetourt County Clerk of the Circuit Court.)

13

Around 1745, Bryan McDonald Sr. constructed his log house at the headwaters of Tinker Creek. The house was set on a high stone foundation and, while rustic, was a comfortable homestead in an area that was still very much the wilderness. The McDonald House is believed to be the oldest dwelling in the county and is located on property now owned by the Roanoke Cement Company. (Courtesy of Gibson Worsham, Virginia Department of Historic Resources.)

In 1766, Bryan McDonald Jr. constructed his own home near his father's. The front is of sandstone and the sides are 24-inch-thick limestone; a rear addition was constructed about 1830. Because of continuing threats from Native American groups, the house was built with a false-back fireplace that led to the basement and an underground escape passage. A late-20th-century renovation retained much of the original character of this historic dwelling. (Courtesy of Library of Congress, Prints and Photographs Division, LC-J7-VA-1403.)

Thomas Arnett recorded the 1786 date of construction of Mulberry Bottom in a stone on the east end of his dwelling. In 1795, when Arnett left the area for Kentucky, the property was conveyed to Frederick Reid. This mid-20th-century image shows the house with rebuilt chimneys and a rear addition. (Courtesy of Virginia Department of Historic Resources.)

The present house known as Stonelea in the Trinity area replaced an earlier dwelling constructed by David C. Cloyd, son of Joseph Cloyd, who moved to Botetourt in the early 18th century. In 1764, David Cloyd's wife, Margaret, and his son, John, were attacked and killed by Native Americans. The stone house, with walls 22 to 29 inches thick, was built in 1799 by Edward Mitchell, a Methodist minister. (Courtesy of Virginia Department of Historic Resources.)

Grove Hill, located outside of Fincastle, was built around 1790 by Gen. James Breckinridge. The massive, two-story brick dwelling had 26 rooms and an unusual plan with two intersecting center hallways. The 1804 Mutual Assurance fire policy for the house stated that the interior was "elegantly finished." The house burned in 1909. (Courtesy of Virginia Department of Historic Resources.)

The house owned by Benjamin F. Nininger in the late 19th century (above) was constructed around 1800 by Jacob Gish. In 1836, Peter Nininger married Lydia Gish, Jacob's daughter. Benjamin, their son, was one of the county's pioneer orchardists and was among those who helped to found the Botetourt Normal School, which became Daleville College, by donating the land for the school and his home for use by the school president. The stone house is now owned by the Bank of Fincastle. (Courtesy of Virginia Department of Historic Resources.)

In 1791, Daniel Brugh and his wife, Elizabeth, came to Botetourt from Pennsylvania and purchased property from Anthony Deardorff. By 1809, Brugh had built and licensed a tavern, located near the historic route of the Great Wagon Road. The log dwelling reflects German construction techniques and craftsmanship. In 1994, it was moved to Virginia's Explore Park in Roanoke. (Courtesy of Jeffrey O'Dell, Virginia Department of Historic Resources.)

Hawthorne Hall, located north of Fincastle, was constructed for Robert Harvey, who developed a furnace on Back Creek around 1787 that became Cloverdale Furnace. The new dwelling he constructed in 1824 (above) exhibited the refined elegance of the Federal style of architecture in its fine brickwork and graceful woodwork. Upon his death in 1831, Harvey left the dwelling and much of his land holdings to his daughter Mary. (Courtesy of Leslie A. Giles, Virginia Department of Historic Resources.)

Eighteenth-century travelers relied on ferries to cross rivers, such as this one across the James River that used a cable and poles to propel it. Looney's Ferry, begun in 1742 at Cherry Tree Bottom, was later known as Crow's and Anderson's Ferry and operated until 1786. Other ferries operated at Saltpetre Cave and Glen Wilton. Ferries were discontinued when bridges were constructed in the early 19th century and transportation focused more on roadway access rather than river access. One of the last ferries in the state was at Indian Rock above Buchanan, which operated until 1948. (Courtesy of the National Park Service, Blue Ridge Parkway.)

Two

Towns and Communities

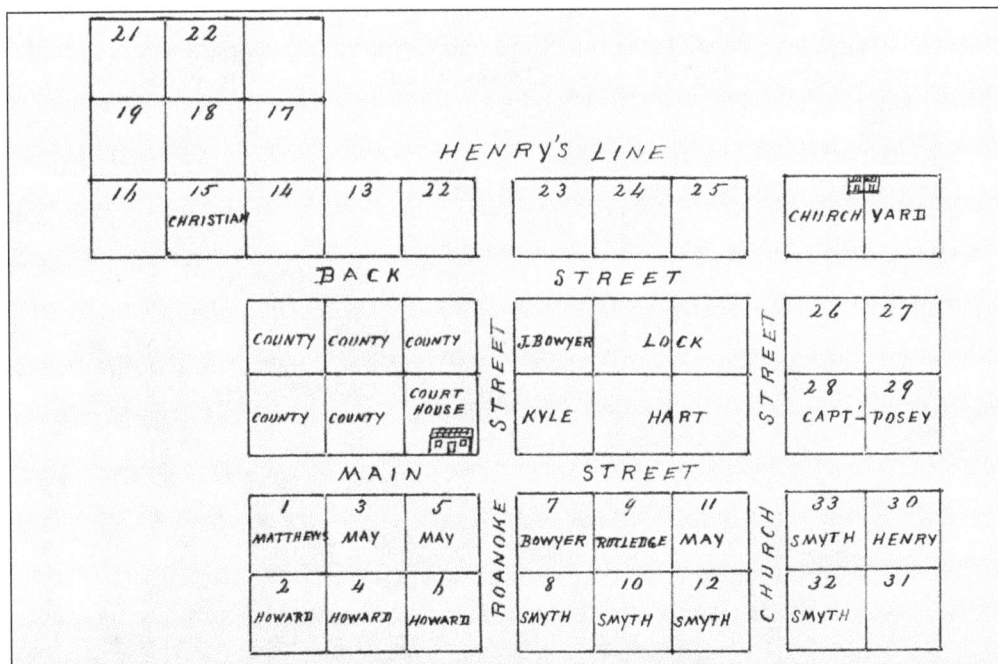

```
 21    22
 19    18    17
                          HENRY'S LINE
 16    15    14    13    22        23    24    25        CHURCH  YARD
    CHRISTIAN

        BACK              STREET

     COUNTY COUNTY COUNTY  | J.BOWYER    LOCK |          26     27
                           S
                           T
     COUNTY COUNTY COURT   R  KYLE       HART  S         28     29
                    HOUSE  E                   T      CAPT. POSEY
                           E                   R
        MAIN              STREET

      1     3     5    | 7     9    11  |       33     30
   MATTHEWS MAY   MAY  R BOWYER RUTLEDGE MAY C SMYTH  HENRY
                      O                      H
      2     4     6   A SMYTH  SMYTH  SMYTH U  32     31
   HOWARD HOWARD HOWARD N              S   R SMYTH
                      O                    C
                      K                    H
                      E
```

In 1772, Fincastle was established as the county seat and named for George Lord Fincastle, son of then-governor Lord Dunmore. Israel Christian donated 45 acres south of the small community of Miller's Mill for the town. This 1778 plat shows the lots that were reserved for the courthouse and for the Church of England. The first meeting of the county court ordered that a "log cabin twenty four feet long and twenty feet wide" be built as a courthouse with sheds on each end for jury rooms. As this plat indicates, nearly all available lots were taken up within the first decade of the town's existence. (Courtesy of Botetourt County Clerk of the Circuit Court.)

In 1773, the first courthouse was completed in Fincastle. In 1818, the log building was replaced with a brick courthouse that was based upon drawings sent to James Breckinridge, then in the House of Delegates, by Thomas Jefferson. The county's third courthouse, shown above in the 1890s, was constructed in 1847 and was based upon the earlier Jeffersonian design. (Courtesy of Historic Fincastle, Inc.)

While building of the courthouse took three years to complete, the first jail was constructed by August 1770. That jail was replaced in 1779 with a two-story log building, and in 1897, a three-story brick jail (above) was erected west of the courthouse. In the late 20th century, the building housed the public library and is now used as county offices. (Courtesy of Botetourt County Historical Museum.)

20

On May 6, 1870, a fire in Fincastle destroyed many of the 18th- and 19th-century buildings from the north side of Main Street to Water Street. The fire, said to have started in the stable of the Western Hotel behind the courthouse, consumed 100 buildings, including all buildings between the courthouse and the Kyle House. (Courtesy of Historic Fincastle, Inc.)

This 1951 image shows some of the additions and changes that were made to the third courthouse in Fincastle, including the clerk's office (right) and the treasurer's office (left). The brick building located behind the courthouse (left) was an early-19th-century law office, later was part of the Western Hotel, and is now the Botetourt County Historical Museum. (Courtesy of NWHP, DLA, VPISU.)

Just after midnight on December 15, 1970, as the county celebrated its bicentennial year, the historic courthouse was gutted by fire. Twelve fire departments from five counties, Roanoke, and Salem were called to battle the blaze. Because of large fireproof vaults installed in the clerk's office and the efforts of the firefighters, irreplaceable historical records were spared in the fire. (Courtesy of the *Fincastle Herald*.)

The brick walls and columns were all that were left of the 1848 courthouse after the fire. Historic Fincastle, Inc., raised funds for the new courthouse, and county taxpayers assumed an $800,000 debt to complete the new building. On Saturday, June 14, 1975, the new courthouse was dedicated. Gov. Mills E. Godwin Jr. delivered the dedication message, and Robert D. Stoner prepared a courthouse history. (Courtesy of Sidney Hunter.)

According to Robert Stoner, the settlement at Amsterdam grew up around the home of George Robinson, who in 1745 was granted 191 acres in the area. Amsterdam developed rapidly due to its location near the fork of the Great Wagon Road, with the western spur connecting to the Wilderness Road and Kentucky and the southerly route becoming the Carolina Road. In 1835, gazetteers indicated that Amsterdam was the site of 30 homes, one store, one church, and a population of 109. This painting by an unknown artist shows the late-18th-century community. Notable in the image are several log dwellings, as well as two churches. In the foreground, a stagecoach follows the Great Wagon Road, which served as the main street through town. By the 20th century, Amsterdam had settled into a quiet village nestled in the heart of the county. (Courtesy of Eugene Crotty.)

SALE OF LOTS
—AT—
SOUTH BESSEMER

A Favorable Opportunity for Investment in Valuable and Attractive Property.

We offer at private sale, and on reasonable terms, one hundred lots in South Bessemer, a locality which is destined by its natural wealth and commercial advantages to become, in the near future, the seat of a splendid industrial development.

South Bessemer is situated at the confluence of the James River and Craig's Creek, midway between Buchanan and Clifton Forge. This creek separates it from Bessemer City, with which it is to be connected by a bridge, soon to be built, so that it is practically an extension of that wonderfully industrial site which is so rapidly attracting the eager interest and investments of the iron masters and capitalists of both this country and Europe. Every natural advantage, every commercial and industrial condition, which assure the success and prosperity of Bessemer City, apply equally to South Bessemer. It is immediately on the line of the Chesapeake & Ohio road, and at the junction of the Craig Valley R. R., now under course of rapid construction, and expected to be in operation by March next as far as New Castle, the county seat of Craig. This road penetrates a mineral region unsurpassed upon the continent for the abundance and richness of its iron ores, while in connection with the C. & O. road, land its connections with the N. and W.) the coals and cokes of New River and Flat Top are brought to its doors, at competing rates. Limestone abounds in inexhaustible quantities. At the village of Eagle Rock, a quarter of a mile distant, four hundred barrels of lime are produced daily. The mountains that environ it abound in forests of original growth, affording every wood required for purposes of construction or ornamentation. All of the conditions, therefore, for the production and manufacture of iron, and for various industrial plants, are here united in an exceptional degree—rich and inexhaustible iron ores, cheap, abundant and convenient fuel and flux, sand stone quarries, railroad communication with the best marts and markets, a healthful and salubrious climate—in a word, every favoring condition for the upbuilding of a great and growing industrial town.

The lots now offered for sale embrace a flat or bottom on Craig's Creek and James River, included between these two streams and Crawford's Mountain. This bold spur of the Blue Ridge rises majestically to the view. Above and below, the sparkling waters of the James are seen for miles; and enclosed as they are by their environment of bold hills, they produce the illusion of a mountain lake, and the effect is hardly inferior to the enchantment of Loch Katrine, so beautifully described in the verse of Walter Scott. Indeed there is no scenery on the Hudson, the Susquehanna, the Tennessee, or the French Broad, which can surpass the picturesque beauty of this spot. The James river and adjacent streams abound in fish—bass trout and other varieties—and the mountains afford a fine field for the sportsman, deer being often killed within sight of the property herein described. Gen. Wade Hampton annually resorts to this locality to indulge his propensity for piscatory diversion, and Grover Cleveland and other notables have been attracted to it by the inducements it offers for such recreations.

South Bessemer is 24 miles from Natural Bridge on the C. & O., and seven miles from Dagger's Springs. A railroad station will shortly be established immediately at this place. The town of Eagle Rock, where there are four or five stores and three churches, and excellent hotel accommodations, is, as stated above, within a quarter of a mile. Mineral springs of the highest sanitary virtue, abound on the premises. These include calybiate and other medicinal waters.

For particulars address.

CHAS. T. PRICE & CO.,
GALA, BOTETOURT COUNTY, VA.

Jno. W. Rohr, Electric Power Printer and Binder, Lynchburg, Va.

In 1890, the Craig Valley Company, a land development group, laid out the town of Bessemer. The town, located at the confluence of Craig Creek with the James River, grew quickly, and by October 1891, some 150 of the town lots had been purchased. The nationwide depression of 1893 slowed the town's progress, and by 1906, only 26 people lived in Bessemer. (Courtesy of Joseph B. Buhrman.)

The Phoenix Bridge over Craig Creek between Bessemer and Eagle Rock is an exceptionally ornate railroad bridge that was constructed in 1887. The bridge consists of an iron and steel Pratt through truss and a steel Warren deck truss and features classical motifs such as a scrolled pediment with detailed vegetation elements, finials, and urns. Built for the Craig Valley line of the Chesapeake and Ohio Railroad, the bridge was converted for vehicular use in 1963. (Courtesy of Virginia Department of Historic Resources.)

In 1779, Peter Flook operated a tavern that also served as a post office and stagecoach stop along the Sweet Springs line. The community took its name from the tavern owner, which was later revised to Flukes. In the mid-19th century, the area became known as Blue Ridge, after the springs resort there. Norfolk and Western Railway maintained a depot at the site of the resort through the mid-20th century. (Courtesy of Botetourt County Historical Museum.)

Around 1840, George Rieley built his brick home (above) in Blue Ridge. George's son Marshall lived in the house until his death in 1928. The Blue Ridge Stone Corporation purchased the house, and in 1971, it was demolished for a quarry for the Boxley Corporation. George and his second wife, Ann, are seated in the front center of this 1900 photograph of one of the Rieleys' family gatherings. (Courtesy of Greg Rieley.)

In 1855, artist Edward Beyer painted this view looking from the Pattonsburg side of the river towards Buchanan. The depiction of stagecoaches arriving in town, as well as several canal boats on the river, are indicative of the thriving economy enjoyed by Buchanan at that time. The covered bridge over the James River (center) was constructed by the Buchanan Turnpike Company in 1851. (Courtesy of NWHP, DLA, VPISU.)

Located on Buchanan's Main Street, the Hotel Felix, also known as Miller Hall, often was used as a meeting place, and political speeches were sometimes made from its second-story porch. The hotel, later known as Central Hotel and operated by the Killian family, was destroyed by fire in 1918. (Courtesy of the *Fincastle Herald*.)

The Hotel Botetourt, located at the corner of Buchanan's Washington and Lowe Streets, was constructed by Jacob A. Haney in 1851 as part of the boom experienced with the arrival of the James River canal. In the 1980s, the hotel was converted for use as a home for disabled adults. In 1997, the hotel was burned by arson, and in 2002, it was demolished. (Courtesy of Virginia Department of Historic Resources.)

This 1942 view of Buchanan looking north shows new sidewalks being installed in front of the Elam house (right) and the Buchanan Presbyterian Church (left). Note the door to the balcony on the side of the church. The bell and clock tower of the Buchanan Methodist Church, which was rebuilt in 1924, is located near the center of the photograph. (Courtesy of Harry Gleason.)

The pedestrian bridge over the James River in Buchanan has been called "the Brooklyn Bridge of Virginia," not so much for its structure as for its fame. A bridge has existed near this crossing since about 1830. It connects the old area of Pattonsburg on the north side of the river to Buchanan on the south. The covered bridge located here from 1834 to 1897 was replaced with a steel bridge and then a concrete bridge in 1938 (to the right). (Courtesy of the *Fincastle Herald*.)

The Buchanan swinging bridge often has been closed to pedestrians during floods and after large storms. In 1985, remnants of a hurricane caused the James River to flood, resulting in significant damage to Buchanan, including the pedestrian bridge, which had to be rebuilt. In the background is the late-19th-century Chesapeake and Ohio train station. (Courtesy of the *Fincastle Herald*.)

Robert Breckenridge's son, James, inherited part of his father's estate in the late 18th century and called his home Clover Dale. Located at the foot of Tinker Mountain, Cloverdale grew into a community with a post office in 1811, a gristmill around 1820, and a Shenandoah Valley Railroad station in 1882. This 1920s photograph shows the two-story school (left of center), the old Cloverdale Mill (top center), and corn shocks in the fields. (Courtesy of Roanoke City Public Library, Virginia Room, Underwood and Underwood Collection.)

In 1847, Peter Nininger built his gristmill in Daleville along Tinker Creek at the foot of Tinker Mountain. The mill continued to operate into the early 20th century and was converted into a restaurant later. Today it is a private residence. (Courtesy of Virginia Department of Historic Resources.)

Situated in a gap between Crawford (left) and Rathole (right) Mountains, Eagle Rock was first known as Sheets when, in 1881, Evan Sheets was master of the new post office there. The town's name changed to Breckenridge, then to Eagle Rock. During the 1880s, the town experienced a building boom that was stimulated by the coming of the railroad (left) and the development of area limestone quarries and iron mines. (Courtesy of Ray and Bobbie Sloan.)

In 1881, the Chesapeake and Ohio Railroad came through the northern part of the county. Eagle Mountain was the name given to the station in the town that in 1888 officially became Eagle Rock. The station shown above was built in the 1880s, but in 1914, it burned. The next year, a brick station was constructed. The frame tower (left) provided water for the steam engines used on the line. (Courtesy of Ray and Bobbie Sloan.)

Eagle Rock, like other communities in Botetourt, has lost buildings and lives to floods. This view from about 1900 shows one such flood. Notable buildings include Emmanuel Episcopal Church (left); the Northern Methodist Church (center); the Eagle Rock School (upper right), which replaced the one-room school seen in front of the Episcopal church; and the railroad station with its water tower (lower center). (Courtesy of Ray and Bobbie Sloan.)

Dirt roads in the county, like this one up Eagle Mountain, made travel difficult for pedestrians, wagons, and automobiles alike. In the 1930s, many of the county's major roads, including Route 11 and Route 220, were macadamized. In the 1950s and 1960s, many of these roads were widened. Between 1960 and 1965, Interstate 81, which parallels Route 11, was constructed through the county. (Courtesy of Joseph B. Buhrman.)

31

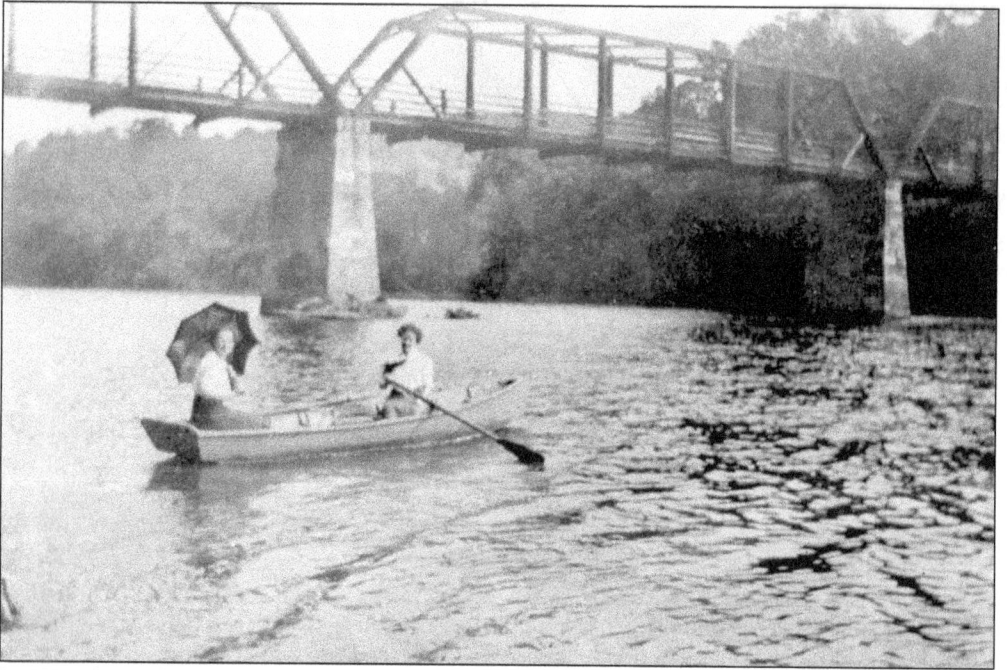

In 1884, the Richmond and Alleghany Railroad, chartered in 1879 and later part of the Chesapeake and Ohio Railroad, agreed to build two heavy timber vehicular bridges across the James River in Botetourt County. One bridge was built in the community of Jackson; the other was located in Eagle Rock (above). (Courtesy of Ray and Bobbie Sloan.)

The wooden truss bridge, also known as the Quarry Bridge, was the main avenue into Eagle Rock from the time of its construction until 1933, when it was replaced by a new concrete-and-steel bridge further up the river. In 1985, Eagle Rock was inundated by floodwaters from the James River. This photograph shows the old truss bridge with the floodwaters nearing the deck. (Courtesy of Sidney Hunter.)

The Gala station on the James River branch of the Chesapeake and Ohio Railroad was the stop for those who visited the Gala Springs and Dagger's Springs north of Eagle Rock. Operated by H. H. Farley, the Gala Springs water was promoted as a cure for indigestion and kidney ailments. The community of Gala lies between Sinking Creek and Mill Creek where they enter the James River. (Courtesy of Joseph B. Buhrman.)

Price's Bluff, near Gala, Va. on line of C. and O.

This 1920s postcard shows the Chesapeake and Ohio Railroad line that ran from Clifton Forge through the northern part of Botetourt County. Here the train hugs the narrow track at Price's Bluff between Glen Wilton and Gala. The James River is at the left and the Rich Patch Mountains are in the background. This area was known for its productive farms and mineral-rich water. (Courtesy of Joseph B. Buhrman.)

This three-piece panoramic view of Glen Wilton shows the town just prior to 1900. Sparsely settled in the 1700s, the community was known as Caroline in the 1880s. The Callie Furnace, constructed in 1874, was the first enterprise to take advantage of the nearby iron ore deposits. When Callie closed in 1884, the Princess Furnace Company opened (far right). D. S. Cook, who was head of Princess, renamed the community "Glen Wilton" after its valley location and his son, Wilton. Princess closed around 1923, and the buildings were removed from the site. Other

landmarks visible in this view include the John Circle house (far left); the Methodist church (left); the Walkup-Givens House (left of church); the Pitzer-Reynolds house "Glen Aerie" (right with fence); and the First Baptist Church (far right), which was moved west of town in 1909 to serve the African American congregation of the Mount Beulah Baptist Church. (Courtesy of a private collection.)

In 1882, D. S. Cook donated property and Corbin Reynolds and others donated funds for the construction of a church in Glen Wilton. Services were conducted for both Lutheran and Presbyterian congregants until 1887, when the church became the Glen Wilton Presbyterian Church. The church is largely unchanged from its original construction. (Courtesy of Antonia Wood McCoy.)

With the arrival of the Chesapeake and Ohio Railroad in the 1880s, Glen Wilton's industrial boom began. The station (above) was located at the north end of town near the iron furnace operations. A spur of the rail line was extended up the mountain behind the station when the TNT plant was built in 1941. (Courtesy of the *Fincastle Herald*.)

Baseball was one of the common diversions enjoyed by many Botetourt communities. In Glen Wilton, a large baseball field with grandstand was erected in the field above town. In the area behind the grandstand, Princess Furnace built over a dozen company houses, which still stand. The remains of the Callie Furnace lie in the mountains in the background. (Courtesy of Antonia Wood McCoy.)

The town of Iron Gate lies both in Alleghany and Botetourt Counties. This early-1900s view looking southeast shows the Cowpasture River as it flows to its confluence with the Jackson River to create the James River. Originally the western terminus for the Richmond and Alleghany Railroad, a track was extended from Iron Gate to Clifton Forge to connect to the Chesapeake and Ohio. (Courtesy of Roanoke County Public Library, Hollins Branch.)

Lignite was an iron-mining community located between Craig Creek and Bald Mountain. The Alleghany Iron Corporation shipped ore from its mines by way of the Craig Valley Branch of the Chesapeake and Ohio Railroad. By 1923, the mines had lost their profitability and the community dwindled. In 1995, the federal government purchased the land formerly occupied by the town and mines and included it within the George Washington National Forest. (Courtesy of U.S. Department of Agriculture, Forest Service.)

This view shows the grid-patterned streets of Lignite around 1900. Many workers' homes were saltboxes, a northern style with two stories in front and one in back, resulting in a gable roof of unequal sides. Lignite had a diverse peak population of 500, which included black and white workers as well as Italian immigrants. The town also boasted a church, a commissary, a train depot, a saloon, a theater, a schoolhouse, and a baseball team. (Courtesy of U.S. Department of Agriculture, Forest Service.)

Lithia, located in the southeastern part of the county between Buchanan and Troutville, was named for the local mineral springs. The arrival of train service in the late 19th century spurred on the construction of homes, stores, schools, a post office, and several churches in the vicinity. Most residents worked for the railroad, at the local lime kiln, or in the nearby iron mines. (Courtesy of NWHP, DLA, VPISU.)

In 1882, the Shenandoah Valley Railroad, later part of Norfolk and Western, built its line through the eastern part of Botetourt County and had a station at Lithia, which prior to that was known as the Back Creek community. The train provided outlets for timber, canned vegetables and fruit, livestock, lime, iron ore, and whiskey—all produced in Lithia. These railroad workers pause at the Lithia station before moving on. (Courtesy of NWHP, DLA, VPISU.)

The Nace combination station, servicing both passengers and freight, was situated along the Shenandoah Division of the Norfolk and Western Railway. This snowy 1917 image shows a few of the railroad workers awaiting the next train. The area was known as Stoney Battery until the railroad renamed it in 1882 as Houston Station after D. F. Houston, superintendent of the Crozer Steel and Iron Company iron mines, which operated nearby. (Courtesy of NWHP, DLA, VPISU.)

In 1883, the post office at the crossroads community (left) also was named Houston for the local mines. It was renamed Mollie for a short period, then changed to Houston Mines, and in 1896, the area was named Nace after George Nace, a local landowner who operated a sawmill there. Black marble was mined on Back Creek and produced black, chocolate, and gray-colored marble. (Courtesy of Virginia Department of Historic Resources.)

Saltpetre Cave near Eagle Rock was named for the nearby supply of potassium nitrate that was mined and used in the manufacture of gunpowder. This early-20th-century photograph shows Gene Allen (left) and Lizzie Persinger (right) in front of the Chesapeake and Ohio small whistle stop, which was built in 1883. Located at a sharp bend in the James River, Saltpetre Cave was a small but active commercial center. (Courtesy of Ray and Bobbie Sloan.)

Saltpetre Cave had been the site of an early ferry crossing at the James River. In 1885, the community included a mill, a post office operated by G. P. Persinger, a store operated by D. M. Persinger, two physicians, a tanner, and two millwrights. This 1920s image shows Joseph Samuel Persinger (far left) standing in front of his store, which was located near the railroad tracks. (Courtesy of Ray and Bobbie Sloan.)

H. K. Allen's water-powered gristmill was located along the Saltpetre Cave Road and was operating in the 1800s. The mill building, shown here around 1920, was standing until the mid-20th century. Around 1889, J. L. Hipes also operated a sawmill in Saltpetre Cave. (Courtesy of the *Fincastle Herald.*)

Located on the west bank of the James River between Buchanan and Eagle Rock, Springwood was established around 1841 as Jackson. Named in honor of Pres. Andrew Jackson, the town became Hickory in the 1880s and then Springwood in 1890. The 1848 Waskey's and Obenshain's Mill (above), later known as Thrasher's, was one of three water-powered mills in the town. Springwood was an important river port for area farmers and later was the site of several canneries. (Courtesy of Ray and Bobbie Sloan.)

In 1884, the Richmond and Alleghany Railroad, later part of the Chesapeake and Ohio, agreed to build two vehicular bridges in the county. Completion of the bridge at Jackson (Springwood) (above) was a celebratory event complete with lemonade sold in souvenir cups. The 1985 flood severely damaged the bridge, and it was replaced by a higher, concrete structure. (Courtesy of the *Fincastle Herald*.)

This 1920s aerial view of Troutville shows the centrally located commercial center with the 1894 Masonic Hall at the south end, the 1916 school (left), and the Norfolk and Western tracks and station (right). The town was surrounded by poultry farms, Kinzie's orchards (upper right), and cropland. Also seen are the Troutville Baptist Church (center), built in 1908, and the Troutville cemetery at the north end of town. (Courtesy of Roanoke City Public Library, Virginia Room, Underwood and Underwood Collection.)

This 1914 photograph shows W. H. Rader (right) and his employees in front of Murray's garage in Troutville. The director's office of Mr. Rader's funeral shop was on the second floor of this building. The bank was located to the left of these buildings. Both the funeral home and the bank later moved to the opposite (east) side of Route 11. (Courtesy of Mrs. E. A. Graybill Jr.)

Three

IN SERVICE

The three sons of William and Elizabeth Rieley—Lewis Harvey (left), Robert William (standing), and Sam Ramsay (right)—joined the Confederate army and fought with the 2nd Regiment of the Virginia Cavalry. Sam died in Funkhouse, Maryland, from wounds received at Gettysburg. Robert and Lewis had returned to their parents' Blue Ridge home in 1864 when Union general David Hunter's troops crossed through the county. (Courtesy of Greg Rieley.)

David Wysong Rader enlisted in Company K of the 57th Regiment of the Virginia Infantry at Saltpetre Cave in July 1861. In October, he was listed as sick in a hospital in Richmond, and in November, he received a medical discharge in Richmond. His discharge papers indicated that he had suffered from the measles. (Courtesy of Botetourt County Historical Museum.)

The Confederate monument located in front of the county courthouse was dedicated on October 27, 1904. The monument commemorated the service of the men who served in Botetourt companies, including the Botetourt Dragoons, the Fincastle Rifles, the Blue Ridge Rifles, and the Botetourt Artillery (Anderson's Battery), and the Confederate women. Botetourt's Confederate veterans gathered for the dedication of the monument, which was sculpted by A. J. Wray of Richmond. (Courtesy of Historic Fincastle, Inc.)

Having enlisted for service, these Botetourt men stood on the courthouse steps prior to departing for training camp for World War I. Among those local men killed in action were Ned Cooper of Blue Ridge Springs; Charlie Dwier, Norwood Fairfax, and Fines Jones of Eagle Rock; and John Rhodes of Buchanan. Others died of wounds received in battle or died from diseases contracted during training for overseas service. (Courtesy of Historic Fincastle, Inc.)

This young man, identified only as "Jim," paused in 1917 at Fortress Monroe to have his photograph taken before shipping out to France with the 60th Regiment, Battery B, Coast Artillery Corps, which was first organized in Roanoke in June 1917. The battery fought with distinction in France and had advanced near the front by the morning of the Armistice. (Courtesy of John E. Alderson Jr.)

Kenton Garland Dodd was the son of Calahill S. and Mary Lee Shelor Dodd of the Pierce Chapel area. Born in 1893, Dodd enlisted in the army for World War I in May 1918. Dodd trained at Camp Lee near Petersburg and sailed to France in August. This photograph of Dodd (left) and Len Bowyer was taken at Camp Lee. (Courtesy of Botetourt County Historical Museum.)

Dodd was among those wounded in 1918 at the Battle of the Argonne Forest in France. His leg was amputated, and he died in January 1919 at age 27. Dodd is buried in the family plot in Godwin Cemetery in Fincastle. (Photograph by author.)

During World War II, civilians were asked to sacrifice and to save materials for the war effort. These Eagle Rock children are shown with the results of their metal scrap drive. The children purchased a war bond with the proceeds. Some of the participants were Buck Dudley (tall boy, center back row), Mary "Paukey" Dudley (far right, third row), Gigi Yonce (far right, second row), Alice Ann "San" Dudley (left of Gigi), and Lib Fuller (left of Alice Ann). (Courtesy of Sidney Hunter.)

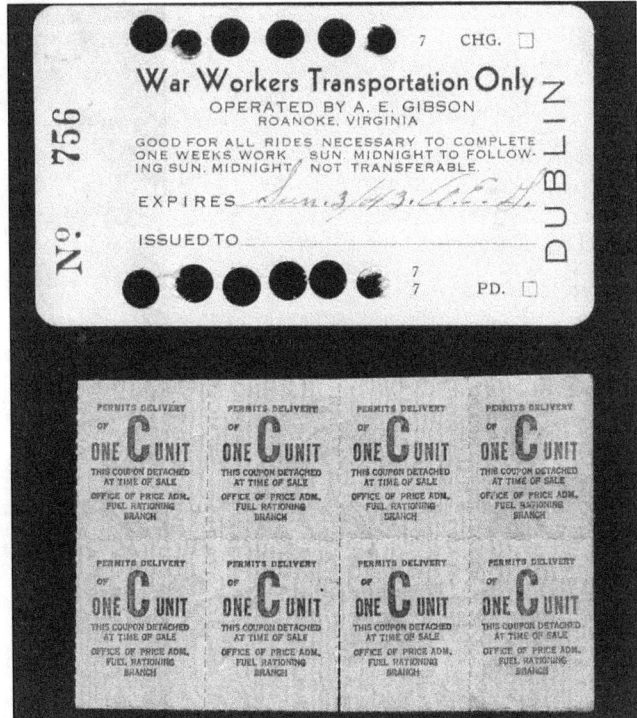

To ensure that scarce consumer goods were conserved, the U.S. government developed a system of rationing that limited purchases of items like sugar, tires, and gasoline. The transportation card (right top) was used to travel from Botetourt to Dublin for work in the ordnance plant. Ration stamps were pasted to each vehicle, which were classified by use, and fuel coupons (right bottom), were exchanged for a limited number of gallons of gasoline each week. (Courtesy of John E. Alderson Jr.)

Eskimo Brown was among the several young Fincastle men who enlisted in the army during World War II. (Courtesy of Historic Fincastle, Inc.)

Clinton Rieley, eldest son of Jerry and Annie Layman Rieley of Trinity, served in Company F of the Central Referral Office Battalion. He poses here (standing) with a fellow soldier in July 1919 in Bourges, Frances. His duties included accompanying bodies of fallen soldiers from Europe back to the United States. Clinton died in 1940 of a brain tumor. (Courtesy of Greg Rieley.)

During World War II, Brooks Edward Parker (right) was in the navy and Ellwood Davis Harris Parker (below) enlisted in the army. Both fought overseas. Their mother was Sarah Parker, who lived to be 101 years old, and their sister is Malanie Parker Jones, a long-standing member of the Fincastle Town Council. (Courtesy of Malanie Jones.)

Known to friends as "Red," Downey Moncure Ware enlisted in the navy during World War II. Red served in nine battles in the Pacific on the battleship *New Jersey* with the 5th and 6th Fleets. Later he received sea command and was made captain of the *Mataco*. Red served three tours of duty in Vietnam and retired in 1975 after 32 years of service as a lieutenant commander. (Courtesy of Botetourt County Historical Museum.)

Maj. Gen. Donald W. Henderson entered the U.S. Air Force in 1960. Henderson, son of Grover and Margaret Henderson of the Trinity area, was awarded the Thomas D. White Space Trophy in 1986 for his "100 percent success rate" with test launches of high priority spacecraft and ballistic missiles and was instrumental in the development of the global positioning system. He died in 2006 at his home in Florida. (Courtesy of Edna Brogan Bolton.)

Four

AGRICULTURE

This 1858 broadside advertised the sale of 300 acres of the John Bowyer estate. Farms in Botetourt were in great demand due to their productivity, mineral-rich soils, and accessibility to numerous springs and creeks. A 1940 agricultural survey of the county stated that "the thick beds of limestone and dolomite found in Botetourt and other Valley counties make the soils of these counties among the most productive in the State." (Courtesy of the Library of Virginia.)

Although the 1960s construction of Interstate 81 destroyed the mill associated with the Brugh farm near Troutville, the antebellum barn is still extant. Built around 1800, the barn is one of the earliest barns in the region. It is a multi-purpose bank barn intended to house livestock and to store hay and grain. (Courtesy of Jeffrey O'Dell, Virginia Department of Historic Resources.)

The Taylor Peck barn was notable for its use of twin silos that were connected by an enclosed and elevated walkway. The early-20th-century barn was located at the north end of Fincastle on the east side of Route 220. It deteriorated and was removed in the late 20th century. The barn has been the subject of several local artists, including William Little. (Courtesy of Virginia Department of Historic Resources.)

In 1871, Dr. Benjamin Elliott Jeter, who married Susan Bonsack, built this barn on his Blue Ridge farm of hewn timbers and pegged joinery. One of the county's best examples of the forebay bank barn, the Jeter Barn has served as a landmark along Route 460 for over 130 years. The old farmhouse was relocated behind the barn when Route 460 was widened. Fourth- and fifth-generation Jeters continue to operate the farm. (Courtesy of Betty Jeter Painter.)

During the first quarter of the 20th century, Botetourt became one of the six leading counties in the state for dairy production. The increased production was due in part to an expansion of population in nearby urban markets and a growth in commercialization—that is, more milk being sold off the farm. The Layman dairy (above) in Daleville operated into the late 20th century. (Courtesy of VCESC, DLA, VPISU.)

Between 1879 and 1939, the number of dairy cows in the county doubled, the gallons of milk produced more than doubled, and butter production went up by an astounding 90 percent. Jersey and Guernsey cows were prized for the richness of their milk, while Holsteins (shown here) produced more milk. (Courtesy of the *Fincastle Herald*.)

Although the average size of Botetourt's farms decreased in the early 20th century, the production of livestock increased due to more efficient farming practices, such as this trench silo used by Brewster Freeman in 1952 for feeding silage to his steers. Beef cattle production peaked in 1920; in recent years, the state as a whole is once again among the top 15 beef producers in the United States. (Courtesy of VCESC, DLA, VPISU.)

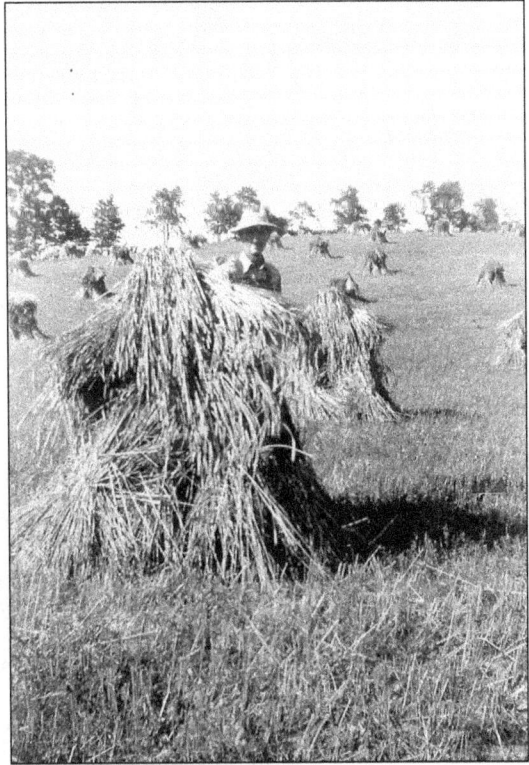

Throughout the first half of the 20th century, the number of acres in Botetourt devoted to small grain production declined, but the number of bushels produced increased as a result of intensification of farming practices and new, higher-yield crop lines. Jacob Alderson stands with his wheat shocks (right), and his son-in-law, Columbus Potter, stands in his oat field (below). Since earliest settlement, wheat has been a major subsistence and commercial crop. Oats were often grown as livestock feed or as spring pasturage, as well as for human consumption. (Top: courtesy of John E. Alderson Jr.; bottom: courtesy of the *Fincastle Herald*.)

In this photograph, Jerry Rieley and his family work in the hay field with a steel-wheeled, horse-drawn, sickle-bar hay mower. After mowing, a side delivery rake was used to sweep the hay into windrows, and then the dried hay was gathered onto a hayrack using a hay loader pulled behind the wagon. The farmer would use a pitchfork to build up the hay load. (Courtesy of Greg Rieley.)

Because of the cost of purchasing thrashing (or threshing) machines for grain harvesting, the job often was done by a local businessman who purchased the machine and traveled from farm to farm with it. This 1880s image shows Marcus Thrasher (seated on the horse) with his thresher that he took to Roanoke and Botetourt County farms. Thrasher also ran a general store in Lithia. (Courtesy of Geraldine Mangus Obenshain.)

Clarence Caldwell, shown at his farm near Flatwoods, operated his belt-driven McCormick-Deering threshing machine from about 1935 to 1950. Wheat was fed into the top of the machine, the stalks were spit out the back, and the kernels were separated and deposited into buckets set in the tray located near the rear wheel. The filled bucket was taken and emptied into a larger container then returned to the box for refilling. (Courtesy of Darys Caldwell Cahoon.)

Before Cyrus McCormick's invention of the reaper, a farmer could cut only about half an acre a day using a hand scythe. His invention lead to the combination reaper and thresher, called a harvester or a combine, that cut off the head of the wheat, blew out the stalks, and separated the kernels. The above image shows a harvester at work on a hill outside of Buchanan. (Courtesy of NWHP, DLA, VPISU.)

Sheep are grazers of forage, and Virginia's topography, climate, and forage resources make it one of the best-suited states in the East for sheep production. Sheep have been on Botetourt farms since early settlement and have been used for lamb and wool. Suffolk, Hampshire, and Dorset breeds are most common in Virginia, but Southdown, shown here in a 1920s herd, were also popular. (Courtesy of Greg Rieley.)

In the 18th century, frontiersmen wove wool with hemp or flax to produce a coarse cloth called linsey-woolsey. This image of Helen Smith of Fincastle taking the fleece from her sheep shows that shearing is commonly done with electric shears, though some farmers still use non-mechanical hand blades. Shearing usually is done once a year. (Courtesy of NWHP, DLA, VPISU.)

Between 1880 and 1940, the number of chickens in the county tripled. As a non–labor intensive endeavor, chickens afforded the farmer numerous benefits by producing eggs and broilers and by eating insects. Although most farms had a few chickens in the yard, during the mid-20th century, commercialized egg and poultry production increased in the county. Here Annie Rieley feeds her small flock outside the family home. (Courtesy of Greg Rieley.)

In the 1920s, Ben Firestone opened a chicken hatchery in Troutville, where he raised chicks from eggs. He then opened a processing plant that employed 60 to 70 people to prepare broiler chickens for market. In 1958, the Firestones sold their company to the Southern States Cooperative. Guy E. Morris (left) traveled to farms to pick up broiler hens for the processing plant. (Courtesy of Ronnie and Melinda Firestone.)

When most county residents hear the name Etzler, they think of country ham. Marshall Etzler, however, had a turkey farm in the Mount Union area of the county, shown here in the 1930s. Turkeys and chickens were raised throughout the county, and many were sent to Troutville for processing. (Courtesy of VCESC, DLA, VPISU.)

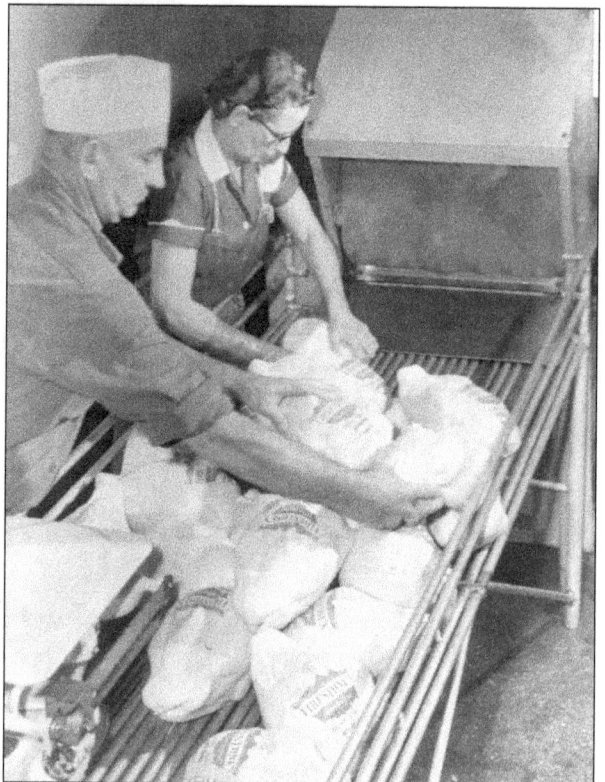

During the 1960s, Southern States employed 190 people at the poultry plant in Troutville, which had a processing capacity of 6,000 broilers per hour. That volume translated into $5,250,000 or 26,500,000 pounds of chicken and turkeys. It took about an hour and a half for a bird to be processed at the plant—taken live from the crate, dressed, cooled, and packed. The birds were marketed under the registered brand Tenderfed, with most being sent to three branches of Kroger stores. (Courtesy of Ronnie and Melinda Firestone.)

By the early 20th century, fruit and vegetable canneries, or "factories," located on nearly every farm in the county, provided secondary income for many county families. The Alderson cannery (above) and the Lucas cannery (below) were located in Trinity. As seen here, black and white workers were often employed at the same factory. The predominant produce canned was tomatoes, although peaches, green beans, and apples were also canned. (Courtesy of John E. Alderson Jr.)

Each cannery had its own commercially produced label that depicted bright and colorful bucolic farm scenes, large rural homesteads, or the items packed inside. The Aldersons' label (above) for their Flat Pond Farm produce shows a fanciful depiction of the farm factory complete with its own shipping port. The Fringer family label (below) shows a typical rural scene embellished with nasturtium flowers. The Fringers operated a cannery in Lithia in the early 20th century. In 1936, siblings Hester and Frank Fringer purchased buildings that were formerly part of the Pulaski Iron Ore Company and operated their extensive cannery from there, producing tomatoes, beans, peaches, and apples until 1950. Frank also bottled Lithia Mineral Spring water and delivered it to surrounding stores. (Above: courtesy of John E. Alderson Jr.; below: courtesy of author's collection.)

In 1924, nearly 125 commercial orchards were located in Botetourt, with most in the southern section of the county. Sixteen apple varieties were grown in county orchards. During the early 20th century, improved transportation provided orchards access to large markets. The Niningers (right) of Cloverdale also operated an applesauce factory. Today the Rieley family orchard (below) is operated by Armeda and Glenn Rieley, grandson of founder Jerry Rieley. The Rieleys produced grapes, nectarines, pears, and peaches. In 1937, Botetourt was one of the leading peach-producing counties in the state and was second only to Albemarle in commercial production. In 1890, Botetourt had 130,000 bearing peach trees, the greatest number in the state. (Top: courtesy of NWHP, DLA, VPISU; bottom: courtesy of Greg Rieley.)

65

The Murray family has been making apple cider since 1924, when a hailstorm damaged Walter Kent Murray's apple crop and he decided to run the damaged fruit through a hand-cranked press. Today Murray's cider can be purchased in just about any grocery store. Brothers Kent (left) and Max (right) continued their father's enterprise, replacing the hand-cranked press with a hydraulic press. (Courtesy of Roanoke County Public Library, Hollins Branch.)

In 2005, all full-time employees at the cider mill were Murray family members. Filling the gallon jars is now done mechanically, but some of the pressing operation is still done manually. Nothing is wasted in the cider process, with apple pressings, also called pomace or "pummies," taken by wagon to the fields for cattle feed. (Courtesy of Roanoke County Public Library, Hollins Branch.)

From its inception in 1882, the Roanoke City Market has been a direct outlet for many of Botetourt's farmers. This photograph shows Earl Alderson and his grandson, John Mark Alderson, at the market in 1969. Earl sold mostly brown hen eggs, broiler hens, and produce, such as the tomatoes in this photograph. The Roanoke market is the oldest such market in continuous use in Virginia. (Courtesy of John E. Alderson Jr.)

Virginia's 4-H clubs began with the early-1900s corn-growing clubs for boys and tomato-growing and -canning clubs for girls. About 1910, similar clubs were organized for African American girls and boys at Hampton Institute. The first 4-H camp was held in Virginia in 1917 in Loudoun County. At first held for girls only, camping grew to include boys and coeducational events. These Botetourt girls attended camp in 1935. (Courtesy of the *Fincastle Herald*.)

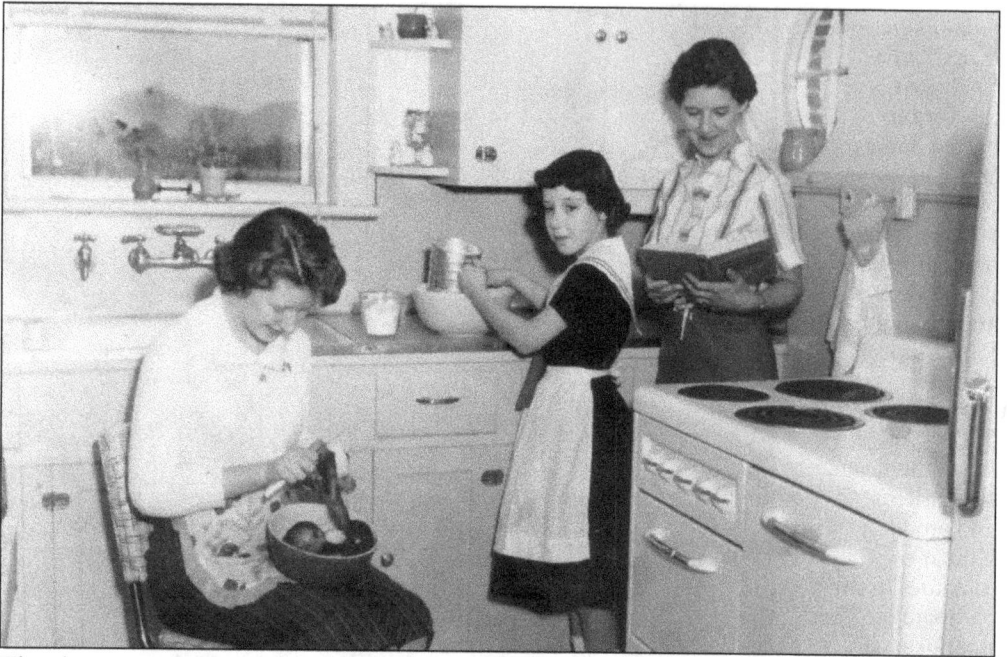

The three Firestone children—Shirley, Bill, and Rita—were all members of the Trinity 4-H Club. Shirley was president, and Bill was treasurer. Shirley won ribbons in meal preparation and laundry demonstration. Bill won a blue ribbon for his sheep at the Botetourt County Youth Fair. Here Shirley (left), Rita (center), and Lois, their mother, are practicing Shirley's apple crisp recipe, which won first place in the countywide 4-H contest. (Courtesy of Rita Firestone.)

At the 1938 annual convention in Blacksburg, Mrs. J. Malcolm (Grace) Peck of Fincastle was elected president of the State Federation of Home Demonstration Clubs. As part of the Virginia Cooperative Extension Service, the clubs promoted basic home economics and encouraged rural homemakers to modernize their houses for improved efficiency and convenience. They often took tours of local homes that exhibited modern amenities. (Courtesy of Culinary History Collection, Prince William Scrapbook, Digital Library and Archives, University Libraries, Virginia Polytechnic Institute and State University.)

The Future Farmers of America (FFA) has been a large and important club in Botetourt County schools for many years. The 1944 Eagle Rock FFA club officers (right) were, from left to right, (first row) Ralph Necessary, Clarence Bryant, G. C. Thompson, Harold Wilhelm, and Jennings Fisher. Thompson established a profitable dairy farm in Gala. The farm now is operated by his son, Richard. (Courtesy of Botetourt County Historical Museum.)

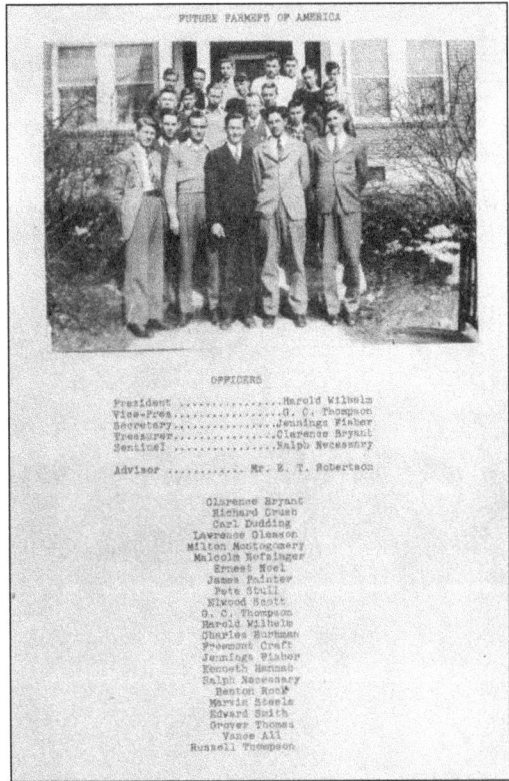

FUTURE FARMERS OF AMERICA

OFFICERS

President ....Harold Wilhelm
Vice-Pres.................G. C. Thompson
Secretary.................Jennings Fisher
Treasurer.................Clarence Bryant
Sentinel ....Ralph Necessary

Adviser .... Mr. E. T. Robertson

Clarence Bryant
Richard Crush
Carl Dudding
Lawrence Gleason
Milton Montgomery
Malcolm Nofsinger
Ernest Noel
James Painter
Pete Stull
Elwood Scott
G. C. Thompson
Harold Wilhelm
Charles Burhman
Freemont Craft
Jennings Fisher
Kenneth Hannah
Ralph Necessary
Benton Rock
Marvin Steele
Edward Smith
Grover Thomas
Vance All
Russell Thompson

Statewide 4-H short courses were annual learning events held to provide educational experiences that weren't available from local clubs. This 1951 Botetourt delegation poses on the grounds at Virginia Tech during their attendance at the Electrical Conference and Atlantic Rural Exposition. The 4-H club symbols stand for heart, head, hands, and health. (Courtesy of VCESC, DLA, VPISU.)

At the 1950 Lynchburg farm show, Johnny Alderson (right, father of the author) and Lacy Smith (second from right) placed first and second in the fitting and showing class with their Jersey and Guernsey cows, respectively. Virginia Kinzie and John Garber also were winners from the county that year. (Courtesy of VCESC, DLA, VPISU.)

Five

Industry and Commerce

The Breckinridge Mill, later known as Howell's Mill, is one of the oldest extant mills in the region. The present mill, constructed around 1822 by James Breckinridge, replaced a mill built on this site in 1804. Situated along Catawba Creek outside of Fincastle, the gristmill operated until damaged by a flood in the mid-1930s. The impressive, three-and-a-half-story brick structure sits on a stone foundation and has 3-foot-deep walls and 20-foot ceiling heights. (Courtesy of Ray and Bobbie Sloan.)

Arch Mill, located on Mill Creek north of Route 11 and east of Interstate 81, was constructed around 1840 by George Waskey. The mill was so named because of a construction arch used in its stone wall. In 1884, Sam Obenshain established a post office there that took his name and was later changed to Arch Mill. Zachary Taylor Obenshain, a merchant and apothecary, and his wife, Virginia Thrasher, served as postmasters at Arch Mill from 1887 until it closed in 1907. (Courtesy of Virginia Department of Historic Resources.)

The Cloverdale Mill, constructed in the early 19th century, was in continual usage until it burned in 1968. The original section of the mill, shown in this photograph, was constructed of hewn beams pegged together. Farmers from Botetourt, Craig, Rockbridge, and Bedford brought their grains here to be milled. (Courtesy of NWHP, DLA, VPISU.)

In the early 20th century, about 30 mills operated in Botetourt County. While the Cloverdale Mill always operated on water power, some mills, such as the Eagle Rock Mill, converted to electric power. The Cloverdale Mill produced flour and various livestock feed by adding different elements to produce the nutritional balance needed for each type of feed. This 1939 advertisement from the Botetourt County Agricultural Fair brochure shows the brands of feed the mill carried. (Courtesy of John E. Alderson Jr.)

5 DAYS   THE BOTETOURT COUNTY FAIR 1939.   5 NIGHTS

CLOVERDALE MILLS

IN SERVICE SINCE 1814

Cloverdale, Virginia.

Do It With Flour of Quality

"OLD STAFF OF LIFE"

A Whole Wheat Patent Flour

EVERY BAG GUARANTEED

LUCKY 4 FEEDS

INDIAN HEAD WATER-GROUND CORN MEAL

We Specialize in Exchange and Custom Grinding.

We Are Distributors For

John W. Eshelman & Sons

GUARANTEED FEED

Phone—Troutville 492B.

The Chambers family purchased the mill in 1931 and added the feed mixer to the north end of the structure. Area farmers brought in barley, oats, rye, and wheat for milling. For every bushel of wheat a farmer brought in, he "banked" 25 pounds of flour and 10 pounds of bran, which was stored free of charge at the mill and "withdrawn" as needed. In 1968, the mill was destroyed by fire. (Courtesy of Virginia Department of Historic Resources.)

Located in Haymakertown, the Catawba Furnace, constructed in 1830 as a cold-blast charcoal furnace, was built originally on a round rather than square plan. The furnace went out of blast in the 1850s but was revived by the Tredegar Iron Works in Richmond during the Civil War. Labor shortages resulted in low productivity, and after 1865, the furnace went out of blast permanently. (Courtesy of J. Daniel Pezzoni, Virginia Department of Historic Resources.)

Located within the Jefferson National Forest along a tributary to Craig Creek, this furnace was constructed in 1832 and rebuilt in 1845. The Roaring Run Iron Works shipped pig iron to Tredegar Iron Works in Richmond. Abandoned in 1865, the original hot-blast charcoal stack of dry-laid local limestone, the wheel pit walls, and the stone-lined tailrace are intact and the stone retaining walls have been accurately reconstructed. (Courtesy of Virginia Department of Historic Resources.)

The Liberty Lime and Stone Company began mining in 1918 at Rocky Point, about three miles below Indian Rock and Edward Dillon's lime kilns. A spur line of the James River division of the Chesapeake and Ohio Railroad ran to the plant. Liberty was later owned by the James River Limestone Company and is now Oglebay-Norton Minerals' James River Operation. (Courtesy of NWHP, DLA, VPISU.)

The Blue Ridge Stone Corporation in Blue Ridge was established about 1914 as a stone crushing operation near the Bedford County line. In 1917, the company was purchased by W. W. Boxley as the fourth quarry in his limestone business. Most work was being done by hand, mule carts, and some steam machinery. The company continues to operate under fourth-generation family leadership. (Courtesy of the *Fincastle Herald*.)

The Eagle Rock Lime Company, located on the west side of the James River across from Eagle Rock, was operated from 1905 to 1950 by James H. McNamara of Rockland, Maine. The Moore Lime Company (above), begun around 1890, was located on the edge of town between the river and the foot of Rathole Mountain. (Courtesy of Virginia Department of Historic Resources.)

James C. Owen Sr. (right) ran the Moore Lime Company Commissary on Railroad Avenue in Eagle Rock. Guy Sheets is standing at the left along with a salesman. The store was rebuilt after the 1917 fire destroyed the buildings along the lower part of town. The store, with its oddly placed radiator, is still intact and most recently was a farm supply store. (Courtesy of Ray and Bobbie Sloan.)

Three beehive lime kilns that mark the northern entrance to Eagle Rock were part of the Moore Lime Company's operations. The oldest kiln, located closest to town, dates to 1847. A group of investors purchased the business in 1933 and reopened it as the Virginia Lime Products Company. The facility closed in 1943. In 1991, the property was donated by Mr. and Mrs. Anson Jamison to the Stoner–Eagle Rock Garden Club for a park. (Courtesy of Joseph B. Buhrman.)

Today the remains of the Eagle Rock Lime Company quarry are located on the western bank of the James River. Most of the quarry work was done manually with the aid of horses and mules, as seen in this 1930s photograph. Among the company's products was hydrated lime for industrial, chemical, and agricultural uses. (Courtesy of Ray and Bobbie Sloan.)

The first restaurant W. W. "Jiggs" Lugar operated in Eagle Rock was on Railroad Avenue near the lime company; it was destroyed by fire in 1917. Jiggs built a new restaurant on Church Street that is now part of Maw and Paw's Restaurant. Jiggs is shown here (right) with two customers in his first restaurant in 1936. (Courtesy of Ray and Bobbie Sloan.)

The Sinclair gas station was located on the west side of the Eagle Rock bridge at the foot of Crawford Mountain. The company's dinosaur logos, including the brontosaurus known as "Dino," were prominently featured on the building. Bill Owen was the original owner. (Courtesy of Ray and Bobbie Sloan.)

In 1907, the Farmers and Canners Bank of Botetourt was organized, and John W. Layman—a Troutville farmer, fruit grower, canner, and grocery store owner—served as the bank's first president. Three years later, the bank reorganized as the First National Bank of Troutville, and Layman continued as president until his death in 1951. The check above was written by bank member Jacob A. Alderson, who owned a farm and tomato canning factory in Trinity. (Courtesy of John E. Alderson Jr.)

The Buchanan and Pattonsburg Savings Bank, incorporated in 1838, was the earliest bank in the county. The Eagle Rock Bank (right) was organized in 1905 with Joseph Benson Buhrman, county treasurer and farmer, as its president. The building on Railroad Avenue is striking for its use of double-height Ionic columns and the federal eagle sculpture above the portico. In 1993, the bank became part of the Bank of Botetourt. (Courtesy of Ray and Bobbie Sloan.)

As part of the continuing industrial utilization of Botetourt's natural resources, the Lone Star Cement Company began construction in 1950 on a plant between Daleville and Catawba. A light snow fell (above) as the construction crew laid the track for a spur line of the Norfolk and Western on November 11. Now known as Roanoke Cement, it is the only active cement plant in Virginia and has an annual production of 1.3 million tons. The plant is one of the top 10 employers in the county. (Courtesy of the *Fincastle Herald*.)

In 1822, Robert Kyle purchased two lots at the corner of Church and Main Streets in Fincastle. Records indicate that Kyle probably built the brick building at this site around 1830. The building (above left), which housed both a residence and a store, is noted for its fine brickwork and its elaborate interior woodwork that includes thistle motifs. Known for a time as Central Hotel, the building was purchased by F. D. Bolton Sr. in the early 20th century. (Courtesy of the Library of Virginia.)

French Davis Bolton married Pauline Aurich, who had come to Fincastle from New Orleans for the summer springs season. Bolton served in the Virginia House of Delegates and owned several businesses in the county. Bolton's sons continued the general merchandise and grocery store until the late 1970s. Since then, the building has been used as a florist, as the Fincastle Baptist Church annex, and now as an art gallery. (Courtesy of John E. Alderson Jr.)

5 DAYS   THE BOTETOURT COUNTY FAIR 1939.   5 NIGHTS

F. D. BOLTON CO.

FINCASTLE, VIRGINIA

——DEALERS IN——

General Merchandise

Kelvinator and Westinghouse

ELECTRIC REFRIGERATORS

Household or Commercial Appliances

Zenith Radios

AGAIN A YEAR AHEAD

Maytag Washers

America's Finest—GAS or ELECTRIC

A. L. Bolton, Troutville, Va.—Representative for

F. D. BOLTON CO.

See Our Booth Exhibit Under Grand Stand at the Fair.

(38)

F. D. Bolton's Chevrolet Garage (above), located on the south side of Fincastle's Main Street, was also a dealership for the manufacturer. Later run by his son A. R. Bolton, the garage became known as the Fincastle Motor Company and sold Oldsmobiles as well. The building now houses Ed Bordett's art studio. (Courtesy of Historic Fincastle, Inc.)

Most county communities had local stores that stocked both general merchandise and groceries. Agee's Store was located in Glen Wilton on the hill above the town. Here Mamie Simpson Wood stands on the porch of the store with her husband, Henry (center), and his stepfather, S. C. Agee (left). This photograph was taken around 1900. (Courtesy of Antonia Wood McCoy.)

In 1941, the Triton Chemical Company acquired land in Glen Wilton and built a TNT plant in a protected area on the mountain behind town. In January 1942, the U.S. government seized the plant for the war effort and placed the facility under control of the Hercules Powder Company, which also ran the Radford Ordnance Works. Known as the Virginia Ordnance Works, the plant consisted of about 20 major manufacturing buildings. (Courtesy of the U.S. Army Corps of Engineers, Norfolk Division.)

Because of safety concerns including a fire, one death, and pollution problems, officials slated the Glen Wilton plant for closure in August 1942. On July 20, 1942, a large blast at the TNT plant killed two workers, W. M. Hill and Lawrence Hipes, and injured four others. The explosion emanated from the wash house (below), which was described by newspapers as "blown to bits." The TNT storage house was showered with cinders but did not explode, which saved the town from certain destruction. (Courtesy of U.S. Army Corps of Engineers, Norfolk District.)

Oscar M. Bowyer's blacksmith and machine shop was located on the Town Branch on the west side of Fincastle. In operation from 1857 to 1928, Bowyer produced fine metal cans and other canning supplies, repaired machines and engines, and could make metal castings at his factory. Note the houses and cornfields behind the shop along Factory Street. An early mill building also can be seen behind the machinery shop. (Courtesy of Historic Fincastle, Inc.)

Originally occupied by Bowyer's machine shop, this lot was later the site of the store built by James Guy Firebaugh. In 1940, Firebaugh sold the store to A. M. Peery and Donna Johnson, who operated it as Peery's Cash Market. In 1946, Firebaugh's son, James Arthur "Ott," owned the store and carried groceries and general merchandise. From 1968 until 1982, Harry Kessler ran the store, which he called "The Fincastle Mart." (Courtesy of Historic Fincastle, Inc.)

Beginning around 1905, George O. Paynter operated this store in Troutville. John W. Layman later was a partner. Taken about 1909, this photograph shows, from left to right, an unidentified man in a buggy, Jack Hipes, Will Rieley, Chris Paynter, George Paynter, an unidentified man and boy on the porch, Marshall Murray, and Thomas Matheny. Matheny was the mail carrier, and the Paynter store also served as the Troutville Post Office. (Courtesy of Bland A. Painter Jr.)

In 1935, B. A. Painter (no relation to George Paynter) came to Troutville and leased the old Paynter-Layman store and ran it a grocery store. In August 1941, the store was engulfed by a fire that also claimed the barbershop and the Obenshain-Griffin garage. The store's former location is now occupied by the Troutville Town Hall and Fire and Rescue building. After the fire, the Painters located a temporary store in the Troutville Masonic Lodge and then constructed the store that now stands on the east side of Route 11. (Courtesy of Bland A. Painter Jr.)

In 1898, Will H. Rader started his mortuary business in Troutville. This 1902 image shows Rader (center) with J. H. Showalter (right) and Charlie H. Rader (left) on the horse-drawn hearse used to transport bodies to homes for viewing and to gravesites for burial. Caskets were made in the undertaker's shop, which was located on a hill on the east side of Route 11. (Courtesy of Mrs. E. A. Graybill Jr.)

By 1914, Rader had relocated his business to the second floor of a brick building on Route 11 that also housed Murray's garage. In 1946, E. A. Graybill, known locally as "June," purchased the business. Graybill, who returned to Troutville after time with the navy, had worked in the funeral home in the 1930s. In 1953, Graybill moved the funeral home to a renovated house, shown here, at the corner of Lee Highway and Stoney Battery Road. (Courtesy of Mrs. E. A. Graybill Jr.)

In 1930, Reuben Hafleigh purchased the former Virginia Can Company facility in Buchanan and moved his bone button manufacturing plant there from Philadelphia. Begun in 1894, Hafleigh's company moved 62 carloads of machinery, equipment, and stock to the new site located near the Norfolk and Western station. A 1936 addition doubled the size of the plant, which had over 200 employees. During World War II, the plant joined the war effort and converted to the manufacture of anti-aircraft gun mounts and parts for naval guns. After the war, the company produced plastic buttons. In 1965, the plant was purchased by the Groendyke Manufacturing Company, which manufactured rubber and silicone sporting goods and industrial gaskets. (Courtesy of Harry Gleason.)

THIS ORGANIZATION IS HERE TO GIVE YOU GOOD SERVICE

HAFLEIGH & COMPANY

BUTTON MANUFACTURERS

BUCHANAN, VIRGINIA

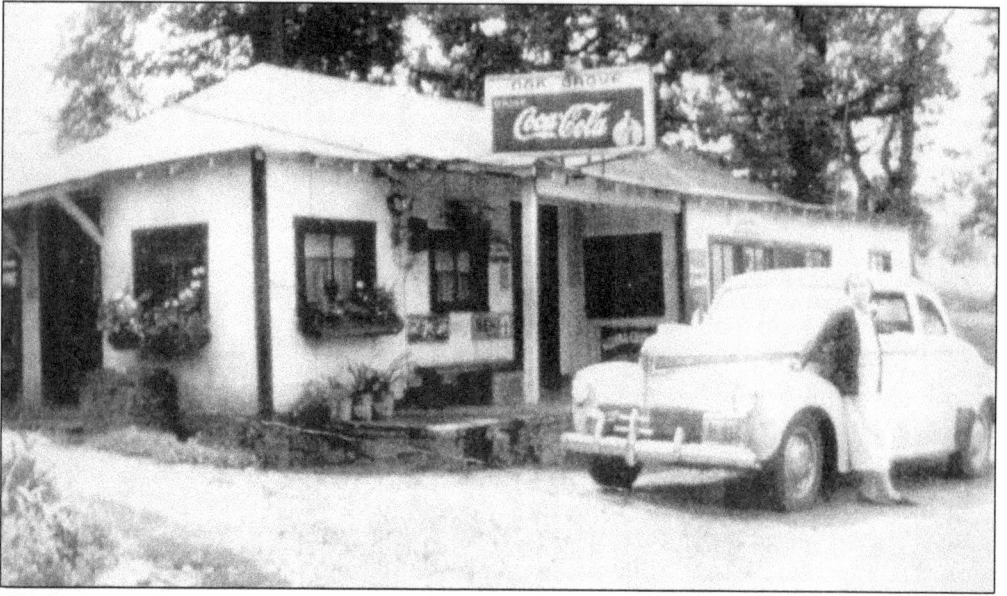

The Oak Grove Tea Room (above) was located in Blue Ridge across from Colonial School. The tearoom was operated in the 1940s by Emma and Joe Swartzel. This photograph shows Kathleen, Emma's sister, who later married James Spickard, in front of the restaurant. (Courtesy of Josephine Zimmerman Noojin.)

First opened in the 1930s, the Mason Dixon Truck Stop was enlarged in the 1960s when highway traffic along Route 11 peaked. Truckers and locals stopped at the restaurant, which was conveniently located just north of Troutville. The truck stop is now operated as Scott's Thrift Store, a service station and convenience store. (Courtesy of Ronnie and Melinda Firestone.)

In 1950, Mr. and Mrs. I. O. Bower purchased the former Northway Diner and established the Stagecoach Motel and Restaurant along Route 11 north of Troutville. This photograph shows Pearl Bower in front of the restaurant. In 1965, Pearl sold the Stagecoach operation but soon purchased the nearby Boxwood, which she renamed the Greenwood. (Courtesy of Darlene Odenwelder.)

This 1952 picture shows Pearl Bower (right) with her daughter Darlene (center) and Ocie Dulaney (left) outside of the Stagecoach. Pearl often had biscuits and gravy waiting on the table or favorite desserts prepared for locals when they arrived. (Courtesy of Darlene Odenwelder.)

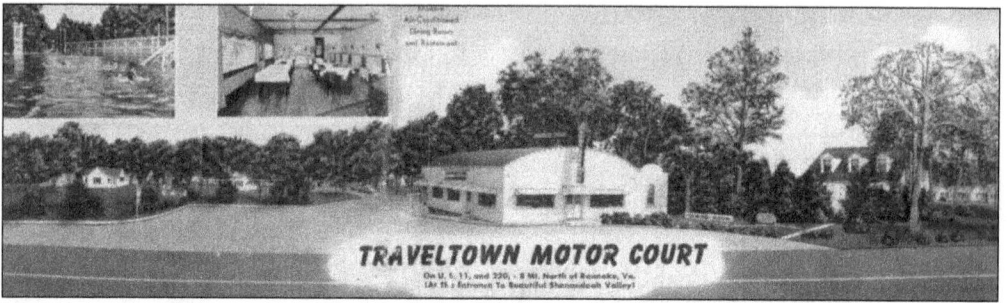

TRAVELTOWN MOTOR COURT
On U. S. 11, and 220, - 5 Mi. North of Roanoke, Va.
(At 11.; Entrance To Beautiful Shenandoah Valley)

Traveltown Motor Court began as a collection of 18 cottages located on a six-acre spread along Route 11 in Cloverdale. Located along this main transportation route and at the banks of Tinker Creek, Traveltown became an annual retreat for vacationing families. Mr. and Mrs. J. H. Jarrett first operated the resort, which included a pool, a service station, and a dining room that served "Old Virginia Ham and Chicken Dinners" as a specialty. (Courtesy of Dorothy Vernamonti.)

In 1930, Traveltown was sold to Mr. and Mrs. Otis R. Buck, whose vision for the site included a modern hotel. The individual cottages were relocated throughout Cloverdale, and a two-story hotel was constructed. The hotel hosted many special occasions, including this Hoge-Bruce family reunion in the 1960s. Dorothy Vernamonti, the Bucks' daughter, managed the hotel for many years, and Sue Thompson ran the pool from 1969 to 1980. (Courtesy of Dorothy Vernamonti.)

Six

SCHOOLS, CHURCHES, AND SOCIAL GROUPS

Prior to the establishment of public schools, education in the county was provided by private tutors and in small academies such as the Bailey Institute in Buchanan and the Botetourt Seminary and Female Seminary in Fincastle. In 1895, Helen Prestlow opened a small school in Buchanan at the home known as Oak Hill. Prestlow sits at the center of the children with an open book. (Courtesy of Botetourt County Historical Museum.)

Daleville College

THIS CERTIFIES

Chester Claude Shelburne

In 1890, the Church of the Brethren established the Botetourt Normal School. In 1910, the name was changed to Daleville College, and a four-year college curriculum was offered. In 1925, the four-year program merged with Bridgewater College near Harrisonburg, and the school became a secondary institution known as Daleville Academy. The Depression ended the operation of the school; the buildings were sold in 1933 and were converted to residences. (Courtesy of Botetourt County Historic Museum.)

The Railroad Academy, first used as a school and church, was later known as the Nace School. Lucian Brugh conveyed the land for the building in the 1880s. A second Railroad Academy (above), built in 1913, was used until 1924, when an elementary school was built in Troutville. The former school was deeded to the Ebenezer United Methodist Church and was used for Sunday school classes. (Courtesy of the *Fincastle Herald*.)

From 1846 until the onset of the Civil War, Botetourt provided a free school system for all white children over six years of age. After the war, free public education was again provided, and by 1906, there were three high schools in the county. In 1914, Buchanan's high school students met in an old bank building in town (above). (Courtesy of Botetourt County Historical Museum.)

From 1901 to 1906, the Buchanan School offered elementary education along with a two-year high school curriculum. Beginning in 1907, the school offered a four-year high school course. The school shown above was replaced in 1917 with the construction of the Buchanan High School on Lowe Street. (Courtesy of Harry Gleason.)

In 1908, students pose in front of Glen Wilton's first school, which was located near the southern end of town. The two-room school was replaced in 1920 by a new brick building on the hill above town. Individuals identified in this photograph include Grace Hambrick (rear center, third from left) and teacher Mrs. Wilhelm behind her. In the 1880s, African American children attended a one-room school behind the Mount Bethel Baptist Church. (Courtesy of Antonia Wood McCoy.)

In 1941, the county sold the Glen Wilton School to the Triton Company as headquarters for its TNT plant. Area residents protested, since their children would have to be bussed to Eagle Rock for instruction. The issue was settled with the closure of the plant in 1942, and the building was returned to the citizens. The school, which still bears Triton's insignia in tile at the front door, is now the town firehouse. (Courtesy of Antonia Wood McCoy.)

This 1916 photograph shows students in front of the Eagle Rock School, which replaced the town's one-room school. The school shown here was located on the hill above town behind the present post office. The first high school opened in Eagle Rock in 1909. (Courtesy of Pat Honts.)

In 1928, the Eagle Rock consolidated school was constructed. The building served both elementary and high school students until 1959, when the county constructed two new consolidated high schools. The Eagle Rock School continued to serve elementary students until 1976, when a new elementary school was built in Bessemer. The Eagle Rock School was demolished in 1978. (Courtesy of Sidney Hunter.)

Located at the corner of Route 220 and Trinity Road, the Trinity School was built in 1911 on land deeded by Joseph Kline Snider. The three-room brick school held grades one to seven, with the students attending high school in Fincastle. The building was similar to others built in the county, with its distinctive cupola, large windows, and covered entry porch. This class, from about 1910, stands in front of the school. (Courtesy of Greg Rieley.)

The Lauderdale School, located on the Wheatland Road near the Mill Creek community, was constructed in 1909 as a two-story building, but remodeling in 1928 reduced it to one story. The 1932–1933 school year was the last held at Lauderdale. Area students were then sent to Eagle Rock. Holding the flag are, from left to right, Wood Williamson, Frank Stevens, and Henry Obenchain. Principal Knoe Brugh stands in the back row (third from right). (Courtesy of the *Fincastle Herald*.)

The first Troutville high school, built in 1905, burned in 1916. The community built another school, which was a combined elementary and secondary school, on the hill behind the present town hall. In 1927, a brick high school was built at Route 11 and Sunset Avenue. This 1929 graduating class stands in front of that school, which today is used as an auction house. (Courtesy of Botetourt County Historical Museum.)

County schools offered a full range of extracurricular activities, including 4-H Club, glee club, yearbook, and, of course, athletics. Here the 1934 Troutville High School cheerleaders show their school spirit. Agnes Rader, Cecil Jarrett, Mary Frances Williar, and Fay Murray are pictured here from left to right. Helen Kinzie is not pictured. (Courtesy of Botetourt County Historical Museum.)

This 1936 photograph of the Fincastle High School faculty includes H. M. Painter (fourth row, far right), superintendent of schools, and E. C. Snyder (fourth row, second from right), the principal. Teachers are Rebekah Peck, L. T. Frantz, Ernestine Myers, Mary Wood, Lulu Slusser, Mrs. Hugh (Blanche) Nofsinger, Mary Myers, S. C. Hildebrand, Nellie Jones, Kathleen Ageon, Rosa Penley, Katherine Smith, Louise Bowman, Annie Payne Lemon, Willie Firestone, Lula Young, and Mrs. E. R. (Myra) Crawley. (Courtesy of Botetourt County Historical Museum.)

When the Fincastle High School burned on April 10, 1942 (above), classes were moved to the Methodist and Baptist churches and to A. R. Bolton's warehouse. The school, built to replace a frame school that burned in 1925, was located on Academy Street where the health department and library now stand. The school closed in 1959, when the county built two new high schools—Lord Botetourt in Daleville and James River in Springwood. (Courtesy of Historic Fincastle, Inc.)

Built for the established Church of England in the early 1770s, this building became the Fincastle Presbyterian Church after the American Revolution. An 1849 renovation resulted in its present-day Greek Revival–style appearance. The building is distinctive for its columns and steeple, fine brickwork, and interior woodwork. In 1942, the Garden Club of Virginia assisted in the restoration of the church yard and gardens. (Courtesy of NWHP, DLA, VPISU.)

The Fincastle Methodist Church was constructed around 1840. The exterior is a well-proportioned Greek Revival–style temple form with Greek key patterns around the doors and windows. On the interior, 10 slender Doric columns support the gallery, or balcony. This late-19th-century photograph shows the church with the old bell tower that was destroyed by a storm and a portion of Slicer-Godwin Cemetery (right). (Courtesy of the *Fincastle Herald*.)

In 1877, some 44 Eagle Rock area residents formed the Emmanuel Society in order to collect funds to build a church in town. On September 8, 1885, the frame Gothic Revival–style church was consecrated by Bishop Alfred Randolph. The church holds a prominent location above the town with a view out across the James River. Despite its declining congregation, the church is well maintained, and special services are held there annually. (Courtesy of Joseph B. Buhrman.)

Though the bride is unidentified, this wedding photograph, taken on the steps of Emmanuel Episcopal Church in Eagle Rock, appears to date from the 1920s. Throughout its history, the church has been available for use by other denominations. At present, members attend regular services at St. Mark's Episcopal Church in Fincastle. (Courtesy of Joseph B. Buhrman.)

Many of the county's German settlers were members of the Church of the Brethren. Commonly meeting in homes, the first Brethren church building was erected in Laymantown in 1847. The Trinity Church of the Brethren (above) was built in 1903 on land from the Joseph K. Snider farm along Route 220. The congregation stands in front of the church around 1910. (Courtesy of John E. Alderson Jr.)

In 1887, the Bethesda Brethren Church was dedicated. The church was built on land donated by George Rieley, who also donated the lumber for the building. Bethesda became an independent congregation in the 1940s, and in 1942, a new church was built with bricks donated by Walter Rieley. In 1946, the name was changed to the Blue Ridge Church of the Brethren. (Courtesy of the *Fincastle Herald*.)

Until construction of a church in town, many families from Glen Wilton worshipped at Locust Bottom Chapel. Both Lutheran and Presbyterian congregations met there. The original chapel, constructed in 1786, burned in 1922. The brick structure that replaced the original features pointed arch tracery with clear glass. Members of the Locust Bottom congregation also started the Galatia Presbyterian Church. (Courtesy of Virginia Department of Historic Resources.)

At their 1920s wedding at Locust Bottom Chapel, Francis Claytor and Homer Myers paused at the tombs of Dr. and Mrs. A. M. Walkup. Dr. Walkup served as a private with the Botetourt Artillery during the Civil War and was among those present in the group's last reunion in 1900. (Courtesy of Antonia Wood McCoy.)

The Galatia Presbyterian Church, located four miles north of Eagle Rock in Gala, was organized in 1886 with assistance from Rev. P. Frank Price. Land for the church was donated by the Haden, Carper, and Thompson families. This early-20th-century image shows the church prior to the restoration of its cemetery and churchyard. (Courtesy of Joseph B. Buhrman.)

While Presbyterians had long worshipped in the county, a church was formally organized in 1834 in Buchanan and met at the Union Church formerly located on Main Street. Constructed about 1845 on land donated by the Boyd family, the Buchanan Presbyterian Church (above) reflects elements of the Greek Revival style. On July 20, 1902, the Confederate memorial was unveiled by Eloise Johnston, daughter of Confederate major John W. Johnston. (Courtesy of Virginia Department of Historic Resources.)

The Mount Carmel Presbyterian Church in Saltpetre Cave was constructed on land donated by John Goodwin and his wife, Eleanor, in 1844. The building, which has been altered very little over the years, is of brick laid in a Flemish bond pattern and set on a limestone foundation. Weekly services are still held at the church. (Courtesy of the *Fincastle Herald*.)

Eagle Rock Baptist Church was organized with 35 members in 1898. First meeting in Hope's Hall in town, the church erected a building in 1901, and a new larger church (above) was constructed in 1923. Mrs. F. R. (Cora L.) Hannah donated the lot for the building on Second Street. (Courtesy of Ray and Bobbie Sloan.)

The Mill Creek Baptist congregation was organized around 1804. At first, members met in a log house on Henry Stair's property. In 1854, a brick building (above) was built on land donated by Samuel Obenshain. Rev. Absalom C. Dempsey was pastor from 1821 to 1867 and is buried in the church cemetery. In 1822, Mill Creek opened a mission church in Fincastle. In 1911, the third and present Mill Creek church was built. (Courtesy of Geraldine Mangus Obenshain.)

Several of Botetourt's Baptist churches, including Zion Hill and Eagle Rock, held baptizing ceremonies in local creeks and streams, such as Lapsley's Run and Craig Creek. The practice is more unusual now, with many churches having baptismal pools built into the altar area of churches. (Courtesy of Earl Palmer Photograph Collection, Digital Library and Archives, University Libraries, Virginia Polytechnic Institute and State University.)

Around 1839, John S. Wilson and Company constructed this two-story brick warehouse on Lowe Street in Buchanan to service shipments made along the James River, which boomed in 1851 with the arrival of the James River and Kanawha Canal. In 1936, Oscar Huffman purchased the building and donated it to the Town Improvement Society, founded by Mrs. Edmund C. (Mary Shelley) Pechin. The building is now known as the Buchanan Community House. (Courtesy of Harry Gleason.)

Originally opened in 1920 as the Botetourt Theatre, Fincastle's movie house was renamed the Castle in the 1930s. The frame building, located at the corner of Main and Water Streets, was remodeled in 1948 (above), and in the 1950s, a cantilevered canopy was placed over the entrance. The theater had a recessed entry with ticket window and a separate exterior entrance (left) to the balcony. The theater was demolished in the late 1970s. (Courtesy of the *Fincastle Herald*.)

In 1965, Mother Maybelle Carter (left) of the famed Carter family of Hiltons, performed at the Fincastle Bluegrass Festival with her daughters Helen Myrl Carter Jones (center) and Anita (not pictured). The festival was held at the fairgrounds about two miles north of town on Catawba Creek and drew major bluegrass acts from around the region. In recent years, the festival has been reorganized and underwritten by Historical Fincastle, Inc., the Town of Fincastle, and the Botetourt Kiwanis Club. (Courtesy of the *Fincastle Herald*.)

In 1945, this group of Eagle Rock women gathered for a day of bridge and lunch in the Salisbury area. The trip involved boarding the train in Eagle Rock, traveling to the Salisbury stop, and boarding boats to cross to the west side of the James River. (Courtesy of Sidney Hunter.)

Around 1910, W. W. Lugar and Addie Worrie were married. The popular Eagle Rock couple was nicknamed Jiggs and Maggie after characters in the cartoon strip *Bringing Up Father*. Jiggs ran a restaurant in town, and Maggie ran the boardinghouse that housed some of Eagle Rock's teachers. Members of the Lugar family still live in Eagle Rock. (Courtesy of Ray and Bobbie Sloan.)

The Spurlock brothers were Fincastle residents who, like many African Americans, worked seasonally at the Homestead resort in Hot Springs. In this 1918 picture, are, from left to right, (standing) Caesar, James, and Edward; (seated) Newman, Meade, and Nathaniel. Their mother was Lucy M. Spurlock, and their sister was Letitia, who married Russell Fairfax. The Spurlocks lived on Murray Street. (Courtesy of Historic Fincastle, Inc.)

In 1959, Nancy Petty (Simmons) was selected as Miss Botetourt. Katherine Harris, who was Miss Botetourt 1949–1950, has identified the contest's organizers and judges in this photograph as, from left to right, Pearl B. Stevens, Fern Robertson, Rosalie R. Dodd, Betty June Cronise Ikenberry, Firestone, Irene R. Sprinkel, Mrs. Malcolm (Blanche) Cronise, and Mrs. William (Josephine) Haymaker. (Courtesy of Botetourt County Historical Museum.)

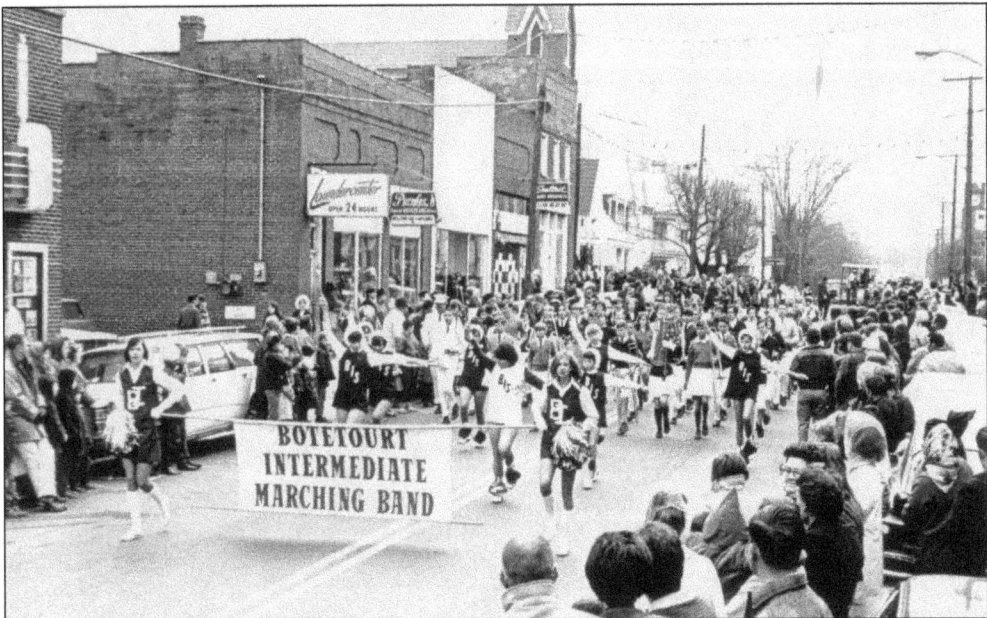

The Buchanan Christmas Parade is an annual event that includes floats, the high school marching bands, and cheerleaders. Other annual civic festivals include Mountain Magic in Fall, a bluegrass, antiques and crafts street festival; and the Buchanan Volunteer Fire Department Fourth of July Carnival. In the spring, the Buchanan Theater (far left), built in 1919 and now fully renovated, is one of the locations for the Vision Film Festival. (Courtesy of the *Fincastle Herald*.)

5 DAYS   THE BOTETOURT COUNTY FAIR 1939.   5 NIGHTS

SINCE 1866

THE FINCASTLE HERALD

The Mouthpiece of Botetourt County

C. H. RIELEY, Editor.

*Can a man be a really good
citizen of his county, and not
be interested enough in the
record of her activities to sub-
scribe to her only County-
Wide News Paper ?*

Right Now You Can Get A Special Rate of

$1.00 Per Year.

(24)

Beginning around 1800, David Ammen published two of the earliest local newspapers: the *Herald of Virginia* and the *Fincastle Weekly Advisor*. Many others followed, including the *Herald of the Valley*, the *Valley Whig*, the *Mirror*, the *Fincastle Democrat*, the *Buchanan Advocate and Commercial Gazette*, and the *Buchanan Banner*. The *Fincastle Herald*, published weekly since 1866, is now the county's only newspaper. (Courtesy of John E. Alderson Jr.)

Members of the *Fincastle Herald* staff in the early part of the 20th century included, from left to right, George Slicer, Claude Hedrick, Charles Oliver, Mose Fellers, and Harvey Fellers. This office was located on Main Street. Later offices were located on Roanoke Street, and the current offices are on Route 220. Clyde Rieley owned the paper from 1932 until 1958 and was the editor until 1970. (Courtesy of the *Fincastle Herald*.)

Seven

HISTORIC HOMES

Santillane, located on the south end of Fincastle, is one of the most romanticized houses in the county. Although commonly associated with George Hancock, the property's history is in fact tied to the Bowyer family. In 1792, the 300-acre property was bequeathed by Thomas Bowyer to his nephew Henry Bowyer, who was a Revolutionary War veteran and who served as the clerk of the court for 43 years. The stately brick house was constructed in the 1830s by his son, Henry Winston Bowyer. The home stayed in the Bowyer family until 1877, when it was sold to Thomas Miller. Robert D. Stoner, clerk of the court for 21 years and local historian, acquired the property in 1948. This view is from Route 220. (Courtesy of NWHP, DLA, VPISU.)

Another romanticized house in the county is Greyledge, located on Purgatory Creek north of Buchanan. The brick house, completed in 1857, was built by Henry Cartmill's sons, Thomas and John, for their niece Ann Sisson. Sisson farmed wheat, oats, and corn with her 33 slaves and also had income from nearby iron furnaces. In 1895, the property was purchased by Edmund and Mary Pechin, who coined the house's name after the limestone outcroppings on the property. Mrs. Pechin, an accomplished author, founded Buchanan's Village Improvement Society in 1903. The Pechins enlarged the house and added outbuildings, including the tenant dwellings known as the Gate House and the Creek House. The Pechins' daughter, Bertha, lived at Greyledge until her death in 1959. Bertha's niece Mary and her husband, State Senator Stuart Carter, then moved into Greyledge, which remained in the family until 2001. (Courtesy of Leslie A. Giles, Virginia Department of Historic Resources.)

When Jeremiah Rieley married Annie Layman, her father, Jacob G. Layman, gave the couple about 500 acres of farmland in Trinity located along present-day Shavers Farm Road. The Rieleys moved into the oldest house standing on the property, which originally was the Shaver family home (below). Rieley raised livestock, grew hay and other crops, and planted an orchard of apples, peaches, plums, and other fruit. The Rieleys had five children (above): from left to right are (first row) Annie, Vista, and Jeremiah; (second row) Marshall Dennis, Clinton Layman, Elsie, and Jacob Ernest. Their descendants still live in the area, although the home is now owned by the Henry family. Many members of the Rieley family, including Jerry and Annie, are buried at the Trinity Church of the Brethren cemetery. (Courtesy of Greg Rieley.)

Robert Price and his wife, Mary, who was from Bonsack and was known as "Mamie," lived in this farmhouse on the west side of the James River across from Gala beginning in the late 19th century. About 1903, Robert was killed in a blast at the lime company in Eagle Rock. In later years, the farm was known as Eagle Valley Ranch and the Blue Stone Farm, but the house was known as Nellie's Rock. P. W. Stoudamire purchased the farm in the 1940s, and the house was demolished. Members of the Price family posed for this photograph (below) around 1930 on the porch of Nellie's Rock. From left to right are A. Nelson Price, Mary St. Clair Price, India Price Murrell (with hat), Mildred Price Huebler, Millie Huebler (infant), and William Huebler. Another daughter, Ellen Norwood Price (not pictured), married Graham McClung Buhrman and lived in Gala. (Courtesy of Joseph B. Buhrman.)

This aerial view shows the Obenshain house located at the intersection of Route 11 and Route 641 (Oak Ridge Road) in the Mill Creek area. Zachary Taylor Obenshain, who was postmaster and merchant at Arch Mill, moved his family from their two-story log dwelling to this large frame dwelling in 1891. Obenshain also built a store and moved his mercantile business and post office to the site. After his death, his daughters and then his son, Carl, operated the store and garage until 1948. Carl and his wife, Lila Magnus, and their daughter Geraldine are shown (below) in front of the garage around 1925. (Courtesy of Geraldine Mangus Obenshain.)

In the 1890s, members of the McKinney family moved from their farm near the Rockbridge County line to Glen Wilton. Two of the older brothers, Tom and Robert, worked in the iron mines. In the 1930s, Willie Radford McKinney (above far right) operated one of the stores in Glen Wilton. Other family members are, from left to right, John Wheeler McKinney, Marion Honts Wood, Lucy Wood (child), Martha Sue Wood, Mary Sue McKinney Wood, Antonia Wood (kneeling), and Lou McKinney Meadows. The house pictured below was constructed in Glen Wilton by Dr. A. M. Walkup in the late 19th century; the small section to the east housed his office. Dr. Robert Givens later lived there, and in the late 1920s, brothers Frank and Robert Calvin McKinney lived there. Today it is the home of Buddy and Diane Wood Buchanan, who is the great-granddaughter of Mary Sue McKinney Wood, pictured above. (Above: courtesy of Antonia Wood McCoy; below: courtesy of Virginia Department of Historic Resources.)

In the 1820s, Silas Rowland constructed the front portion of his two-story brick home known as Wheatland Manor. In the 1850s, Rufus Pitzer, a deputy sheriff, built the two-story front porch onto the house and added a two-story brick ell. While the exterior was modified to reflect the newly popular Greek Revival style, the interior retained its original Federal-style elements. In the late 19th century, the farm was owned by Jacob Cronise, a cattle farmer whose family helped to establish the Wheatland Lutheran Church in the late 1880s. In the early 20th century, the Williamson family operated a Grade C dairy and a tomato cannery there and grew wheat and corn. The National Register nomination for Wheatland Manor states that it is one of the most architecturally refined and best preserved antebellum plantation houses in the county and that its front porch is "without match." (Courtesy of J. Daniel Pezzoni, Virginia Department of Historic Resources.)

Cherry Tree Bottom is located at the bend of the James River between Looney's and Purgatory Creeks, north of Buchanan. In the 1700s, the land was owned by James Patton and passed to his son-in-law, John Buchanan. In 1848, Joseph Schultz, a contractor with the James River and Kanawha Canal, built a home there. The family of local historian Harry Fulwiler (seated in high chair, about 1905) purchased the property in 1890. (Courtesy of the *Fincastle Herald*.)

Mary Johnston, daughter of Confederate major John W. Johnston and Elizabeth Alexander, was born in Buchanan in 1870. Mary became one of the best-known writers of her day and was critically acclaimed for her historical romances, which were often set in Virginia. Her Buchanan home, shown here in the early 20th century, sat across from the Wilson Warehouse. The Johnston house burned in 1972 and soon after was demolished. (Courtesy of Harry Gleason.)

Eight

THE NATURAL
RESOURCES

The James River is formed in Botetourt County about one-half mile below Iron Gate at the confluence of the Cowpasture and the Jackson Rivers and flows to the Chesapeake Bay at Hampton Roads. It snakes generally southward through the county until it strikes the base of the Blue Ridge Mountains above Buchanan, where it rounds Purgatory Mountain and flows almost due east. The river has always been an important transportation route, and by the 1800s, the James River and Kanawha Canal was proposed as a way to link the James with western rivers. Work began on the canal in Richmond and reached Buchanan in 1851. Tunnels and locks then were constructed between Buchanan and Eagle Rock, but the Civil War interrupted the work, and railroads replaced the river as the main freight route. This image shows the river on a summer afternoon from the Glen Wilton bridge. (Photograph by author.)

This 1920s group of ring jousters met in a Bessemer hayfield to perform their game of skill, in which the horsemen with lances attempted to thread a suspended brass ring while riding at full speed. Rathole Mountain and the old railroad bridge can be seen behind the group. Among those pictured are, from left to right, Burt Nichols, unidentified, ? Hope, Herbert Spiller, George Nichols, Jack Seay, Hubert Gattlin, Blair Speller, unidentified, and James McNamara. (Courtesy Ray and Bobbie Sloan.)

No youngster in the county misses public pools in the summer, when cool creeks flow nearby. It is not uncommon to find rope swings hanging from trees along Craig Creek, Jennings Creek, and even the James River. (Courtesy of the *Fincastle Herald*.)

Fincastle's Big Spring is located east of the Presbyterian church on part of the land that was granted to Israel Christian and was included in his original donation of land for the town. The original springhouse was replaced in 1895 by a stone structure that is still standing (above). The Big Spring Garden Club maintains the park. (Courtesy of the *Fincastle Herald*.)

By the 1870s, Fincastle experienced an influx of visitors who came to partake of the lithiated ferro-magnesian spring water that was said to cure digestive disorders and other ailments. William B. Hayth's hotel on Roanoke Street was a popular destination for springs visitors. Offering such amenities as a millinery shop and a photographic studio, the hotel accommodated 150 people. The hotel closed in the 1930s. (Courtesy of Botetourt County Historical Museum.)

Soon after the Civil War, John McDaniels developed the Blue Ridge Springs resort. With its mountain scenery, easy rail access, and medicinal waters, the hotel was a great success. In the 1880s, owner Phil Brown constructed a new hotel with 180 rooms and three multi-roomed cottages. Even with the added space, the hotel was known to turn away guests during the busy season. The hotel burned in the late 1930s. (Courtesy of Josephine Zimmerman Noojin.)

The Daggers Springs resort consisted of about 18 cottages. The springs advertisements promised iron and sulphur water along with "fishing, hunting and dry air." Today nothing remains of the resort located east of Gala. This group visited the springs on July 4, 1907. James C. Owens II, born in 1905 and still living in Eagle Rock, has identified himself as the baby at the front center of this photograph. (Courtesy of the *Fincastle Herald*.)

Begun in the 1930s as a New Deal project, the Blue Ridge Parkway stretches along the crest of the Blue Ridge Mountains. In Botetourt, the parkway travels northeast to southwest through the eastern portion of the county. While the natural scenery is the main attraction of the parkway, stonework like this tunnel also illustrates the man-made artistry of the Italian and Spanish immigrant stonemasons who worked on the project. (Courtesy of National Park Service, Blue Ridge Parkway.)

Limited access and no commercial signage help the parkway retain its scenic charm. This 1940s view looking towards the Peaks of Otter shows the roadway just prior to paving. The parkway connects the Great Smoky Mountains in the south to the Shenandoah National Park in the north. The nearly 500-mile road consists of sharp turns, majestic overviews, and trips through verdant valleys. (Courtesy of National Park Service, Blue Ridge Parkway.)

On July 4, 1927, the Church of the Brethren dedicated Camp Bethel, its youth conference camp located between Lithia and Nace. Once part of the large farm owned by John Graybill in the 1780s, the camp held weekly camps for youth and leadership training. In the 1970s, additional land was purchased, accreditation was received, and a year-round staff was hired. In 2005, church leaders held a rededication service at the camp. (Courtesy of Camp Bethel.)

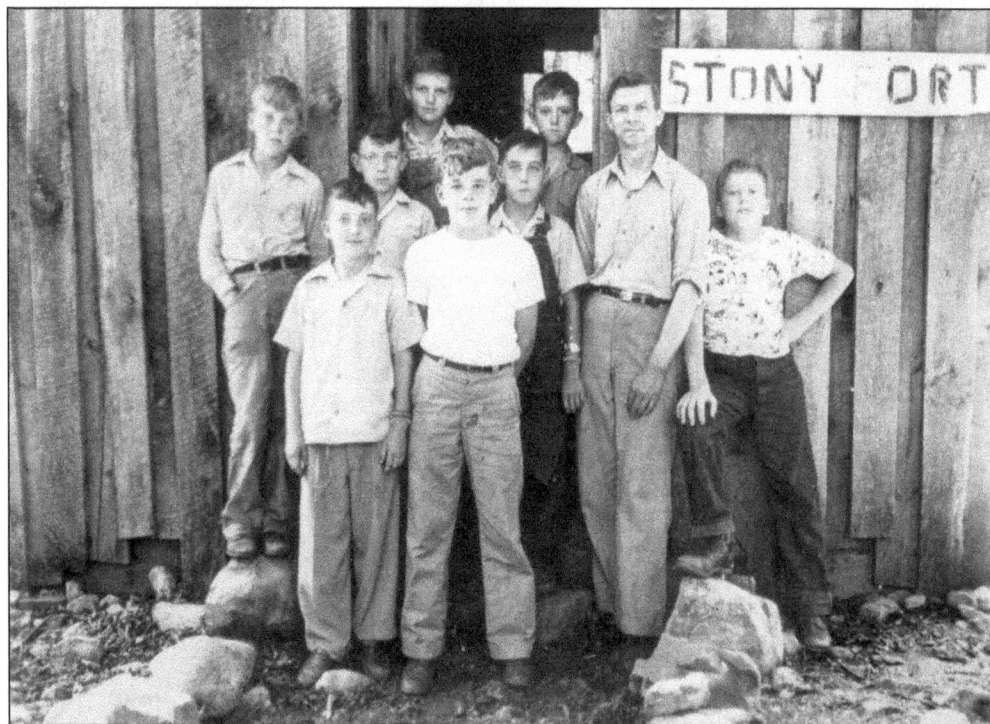

Bethelites stayed in one of the nine rustic log cabins equipped with bunk beds. Each year, campers made scrapbooks that contained photographs, details on classes and events, and personal remembrances from the week. The scrapbooks were decorated and bound, and most have been preserved by Camp Bethel. (Courtesy of Camp Bethel.)

124

In 1933, these intrepid campers, carrying their evening meal, were prepared for a nature hike up the mountain along the old turnpike route. The two-hour hike took them up a dried creek bed to the top of the mountain and over to the other side "to see the view." Along the hike, they also studied rocks, trees, and wildlife. The camp now encompasses nearly 500 acres of rugged beauty. (Courtesy of Camp Bethel.)

This 1932 group of campers anticipated a dip in the newly completed, spring-fed pool. The afternoons afforded leisure, and in the evening, vespers and camp songs ended the day.

In the hills of old Virginia
Where the whippoorwills are calling
And the crystal streams are flowing
Is our Camp Bethel.

There is play and thought and study
There is friendship true and tender
There is worship morn and evening
In Our Camp Bethel.
        —Camp Bethel Hymn, 1927
(Courtesy of Camp Bethel.)

Harry Fulwiler Jr. in his history of Buchanan states that Purgatory Mountain and the creek of the same name were so called by early German settlers because the area around them were "hell to get through." In 1999, Purgatory seemed to live up to its name as a large fire broke out and burned over 1,200 acres on the ridge. The mountain presents a majestic air in this foggy portrait. (Courtesy of the *Fincastle Herald*.)

The figure of Tinker Mountain in the southern end of the county is another of the natural landmarks that distinguish the county's landscape. The Appalachian Trail crosses the crest of Tinker, and from its height, Carvin's Cove Reservoir is visible to the south. This image captures the pastoral beauty of the county. (Courtesy of NWHP, DLA, VPISU.)

BIBLIOGRAPHY

About Town: A Pictorial Review of Old Fincastle, Virginia. Fincastle, VA: Historic Fincastle, Inc., 1990.

Barber, Michael B., Michael F. Barber, Christopher L. Bowen, and P. Brian Huba. *The Phase II Archaeological Evaluations of Two Historic Homesteads and Three Prehistoric Camps at the Botetourt Center at Greenfield, Botetourt County, Virginia.* Prepared for Botetourt County Board of Supervisors. Copy on file at the Virginia Department of Historic Resources, Archives, Richmond, Virginia, 1998.

Botetourt Heritage Book Committee. *Botetourt County, Virginia, Heritage Book, 1770–2000.* Summersville, WV: Walsworth Publishing Company, Inc., 2001.

Bowman, Paul Haynes. *Brethren Education in the Southeast: An Account of the Educational Endeavors among the Brethren People in the Southeastern Region 1857–1955.* Bridgewater, VA: Bridgewater College, 1955.

Cohen, Irwin B., Robert N. Gilliam, William H. Hodill, et al. *An Economic and Social Survey of Botetourt County.* A laboratory research study in the School of Rural Social Economics of the University of Virginia. Charlottesville: University of Virginia, 1942.

Crotty, A. Eugene. *The Visits of Lewis and Clark to Fincastle, Virginia: Why was a Montana River Named for a Fincastle Girl?* Roanoke: The History Museum and Historical Society of Western Virginia, 2003.

Fulwiler, Harry Jr. *Buchanan, Virginia: Gateway to the Southwest.* Radford, VA: Commonwealth Press, 1980.

Jones, Allie Sloss. *Amid the Great Valley: Oriskany.* Oriskany, VA: Oriskany Press, 2002.

Kagey, Deedie Dent. *Community at the Crossroads: A Study of the Village of Bonsack of the Roanoke Valley.* Roanoke: Privately Published by D. D. Kagey, 1983.

Niederer, Frances J. *The Town of Fincastle, Virginia.* Charlottesville: University Press of Virginia, 1965.

Obenshain, Mary Anne, and Rosalie Hamilton Goad. *Town of Troutville, Virginia: A History of Early Years.* Roanoke: Privately Published by Mary Anne Obenshain and Rosalie Hamilton Goad, 2002.

Prillaman, Helen R. *Places Near the Mountains: From the Community of Amsterdam, Virginia, up the Road to Catawba, on Waters of the Catawba and Tinker Creeks, along the Carolina Road as it Approached Big Lick and other Areas, Primarily North Roanoke.* Roanoke: Privately Published by H. R. Prillaman, 1985.

Stoner, Robert Douthat. *A Seed-Bed of the Republic: A Study of the Pioneers in the Upper (Southern) Valley of Virginia.* Roanoke: Roanoke Historical Society, 1962.

Vassar, Stephen D. Sr. *Life Along Back Creek and Looney's Mill Creek: the Lithia and Mill Creek Sections of Botetourt County, Virginia.* Roanoke: Privately Published by S. D. Vassar, 2001.

Wheat, I. David Jr. *Becoming Bank of Botetourt: Centennial Celebration of a Community Bank, 1899–1999.* Roanoke: Dominion Solutions, Inc., 1999.

DISCOVER THOUSANDS OF LOCAL HISTORY BOOKS FEATURING MILLIONS OF VINTAGE IMAGES

Arcadia Publishing, the leading local history publisher in the United States, is committed to making history accessible and meaningful through publishing books that celebrate and preserve the heritage of America's people and places.

Find more books like this at
www.arcadiapublishing.com

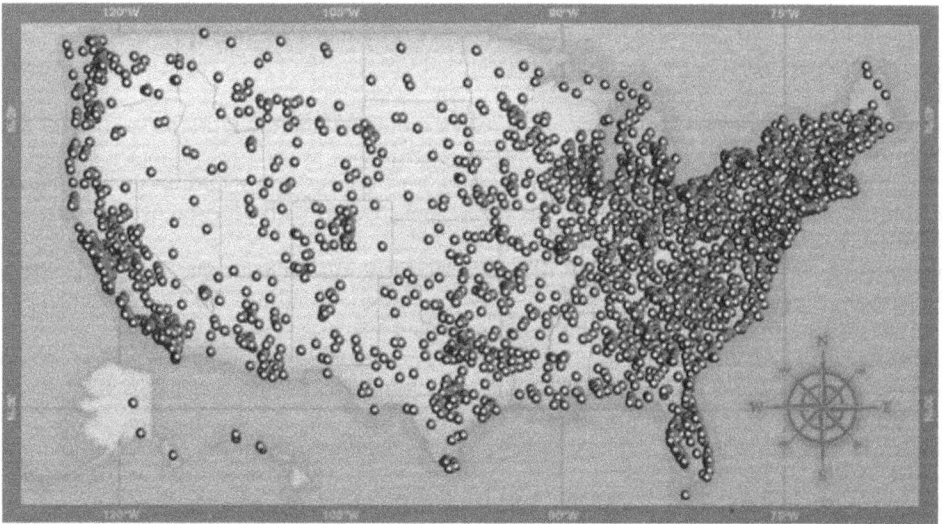

Search for your hometown history, your old stomping grounds, and even your favorite sports team.

Consistent with our mission to preserve history on a local level, this book was printed in South Carolina on American-made paper and manufactured entirely in the United States. Products carrying the accredited Forest Stewardship Council (FSC) label are printed on 100 percent FSC-certified paper.

MADE IN THE USA

www.ingramcontent.com/pod-product-compliance
Lightning Source LLC
Chambersburg PA
CBHW080601110426
42813CB00006B/1373